WHY WAIT?

Josh McDowell

HOW TO HELP
YOUR CHILD SAY

"NO"

TO SEXUAL
PRESSURE

Josh McDowell

HOW TO HELP
YOUR CHILD SAY

"NO"

TO SEXUAL
PRESSURE

WORD PUBLISHING

Word (UK) Ltd
Milton Keynes, England

WORD AUSTRALIA
Heathmont, Victoria, Australia
SUNDAY SCHOOL CENTRE WHOLESALE
Salt River, South Africa
ALBY COMMERCIAL ENTERPRISES PTE LTD
Balmoral Road, Singapore
CONCORDE DISTRIBUTORS LTD
Havelock North, New Zealand
CROSS (HK) CO
Hong Kong

HOW TO HELP YOUR CHILD SAY NO TO SEXUAL PRESSURE

ISBN 0–85009–150–0

Reproduced, printed and bound in Great Britain for Word (UK) Ltd by Cox and Wyman Ltd, Reading.

To

Dick Day

. . . a man I admire and love. His insights as a Family, Marriage and Child counselor has impacted me and my family.

This book would not be possible without Dick's input into our family. You might say, "He is a co-author."

Josh

Acknowledgments

The completion of any book is a cooperative effort and this one is no exception. I am deeply indebted to Larry Stone and Larry Weeden for their significant contribution to this book. Their insights, writing skills and dedication to me and this project deserves special thanks. I want to acknowledge Joey Paul, Vice-President, Educational Products Division of Word, Inc., who has devoted himself to this and the entire "WHY WAIT?" project beyond the call of duty. Also my thanks to Al Bryant, Managing Editor of Word, Inc., and to Dave Bellis, National Director of "WHY WAIT?" for their work in the final readying of the manuscript. My thanks ultimately go to God who has given me my wife, Dottie, and our four lovely children with whom to share the principles found in this book.

Julian, CA   *Josh McDowell*
August 3, 1987

Contents

1 ☿

The Adolescent Sexuality Crisis

LISTEN TO THE WORDS of a teenage girl who, at age 13, gave in to the pressure to engage in sexual intercourse—an all-too-common occurrence today:

> . . . Having premarital sex was the most horrifying experience of my life. It wasn't at all the emotionally satisfying experience the world deceived me into believing. I felt as if my insides were being exposed and my heart left unattended . . . . I know God has forgiven me of this haunting sin, but I also know I can never have my virginity back. I dread the day that I have to tell the man I truly love and wish to marry that he is not the only one, though I wish he were . . . I have stained my life—a stain that will never come out.
>
> *Monica*

America's teenagers are in crisis today. Like me, the father of four children, you probably wish it weren't so, and you might even prefer to pretend it just isn't true. But it is. And if we as parents are going to be able to help our children—and we can be a *tremendous* help to our children—we dare not bury our heads in the sand. We must learn about this crisis and what can be done to win the battle. That's what this book is all about.

The Startling Facts

The crisis to which I refer is the adolescent sexuality dilemma, and it's a huge problem. A 1981 Guttmacher Institute study showed that by age twenty, 81 percent of unmarried males and 60 percent of unmarried females have engaged in sexual intercourse. These young people are becoming sexually active as early as age eleven. And that was in 1981! In the last twenty years, the rate of premarital sexual intercourse has soared through the roof.

Lest we assume, as Christian parents, that our children are safe because of their faith and church involvement, we should be aware that while "religion-conscious" girls are 86 percent more likely to say it's important to be a virgin at marriage than "non-religion-conscious" girls, those same religion-conscious girls are only *14 percent* more likely to actually *be* virgins. Thus, being active in church is no guarantee that a young person is immune to the pressures pushing teens into premarital sexual involvement.

Understand, too, that it's not just puritanical parents who think rampant teenage sexual activity is a problem. In a 1986 poll conducted for *Teenage* magazine, teens themselves identified it as the number one problem they face. Other serious problems like drug abuse, alcoholism, and suicide were all ranked by the teens *below* premarital sexual relations as serious concerns.

Teenage sexual activity results in many problems. The most obvious result is teen pregnancy. More than one million teenage girls become pregnant each year, four out of five of them unmarried—30,000 under the age of fifteen. Seventy percent of the unwed teenage mothers will go on welfare; many of them, of course, opt for an abortion rather than carrying their children to full term.

Further, of those teenage girls who marry because of pregnancy, 60 percent will be divorced within five years. And 60 percent of those girls will be pregnant again within two years. The simple fact is that many teens' lives are ruined—both girls and boys—by pregnancy resulting from premarital sex.

Another obvious problem is sexually transmitted diseases (STDs). These are spreading like wildfire because of promiscuity. Syphilis and gonorrhea are still with us, and newly discovered diseases like herpes, chlamydia, and AIDS (Acquired Immune Deficiency Syndrome) are spreading rapidly. The Federal Centers for Disease Control say the nation is in the grip of an STD epidemic.

Less obvious but just as real are other damaging consequences of premarital sex: feelings of guilt, low self-esteem, being used, wondering if a future spouse will understand and forgive (like the girl quoted at the beginning of this chapter), disillusionment with sex and relationships, and even the prospect of future marriage.

It's no wonder that teens themselves recognize how serious the problem is.

The Challenge of Parenting

If all these facts tend to make you despair that anything can be done to stem the tide, don't give up hope. Parenting may not always be easy, but it can be one of the most wonderful experiences on earth. There are more challenges today than ever, but it's not something to suffer through. Being a parent is something to enjoy as you watch your children grow and develop. It is one of my greatest joys in life. As parents we must pull together and encourage one another.

My own motivation to learn about parenting—and eventually to write this book—came out of a situation that occurred when my third child, Katie, was born. I was in the delivery room and the nurse handed her to me. I panicked, and tears started coming to my eyes. I prayed, "God, help me, I'm a parent again." I had never been trained to be a parent. My parents didn't really love each other. They didn't have a marriage; they had an existence together. I never once saw my father hug my mother, let alone spend time with her. Neither did he spend time with me. I never knew what positive parenting was, and in that hospital room I panicked. As a result of that anxiety I started to pray and ask God to give me wisdom to build a family that would honor and glorify Him.

Parenting takes work, but the work brings results. Clearly we parents should be involved in trying to help our kids. We can't count on society or the public schools, and the church can't do it alone. But the good news is that we parents *can* assist. We have a responsibility and an opportunity to help them say no to the pressures they face to take part in premarital sex. They may not act as if they want our aid because one of the forces at work in a teenager's life is that he or she is becoming an independent person. They are separating themselves from their parents and that usually involves pushing away. And we must gradually release them. But in spite of that, teenagers have told me repeatedly that they would prefer to learn about sex from their parents.

In fact, Utah State University sociologist Brent Miller discovered that the more openly parents talked to their teens about their sex-related values and beliefs, the less active their kids were in sexual behavior. Also, if the teens learned the sexual facts from their parents, they were significantly less likely to be sexually active than those who learned such information from friends.

Ideally, instilling the values and strength of character that will help an adolescent remain morally clean begins at a very early age, and we'll discuss in this book what we should teach at what ages. In fact, I have learned that you should start rearing your teenager before he or she is born. What I mean by that is you should start before birth to prepare yourself to be a model for your child.

But even if your child is now a teen and you know you haven't done the job you should have in his or her early years, it's never too late to start. Your job will be more difficult than if you'd started earlier, but by no means is it impossible.

This book is written from the premise that the Bible teaches sex is a great gift from God, a wonderful thing as long as it's part of a loving marriage relationship. In any other context, it's wrong. It's wrong because God says it's wrong, which ought to be reason enough by itself, but it's also wrong because it inevitably leads to emotional and psychological harm.

Thus, the best answer to the adolescent sexuality crisis isn't better sex education, as important as that is. It definitely isn't widespread distribution of condoms. Rather, it's teaching kids to say no to the pressures to get involved and helping them see that waiting is the best choice they can make. I have dealt extensively with why a young person should wait in my book, *Why Wait?* There I examine thirty-seven reasons why young people have premarital sex and twenty-seven reasons to wait.

There Is Hope

This book is divided into two major parts. In the first, we'll look at the root causes of our present crisis, the pressures that are at work on your child to become sexually active and why teens give in to those pressures. In Part II, we'll look at some specific steps in effectively treating those causes, ways to help your child say no to those pressures.

As parents, we have a responsibility to our children. If you know your child is doing something he or she shouldn't, that knowledge can produce in you a lot of guilt, as well as despair. But we need to keep three facts squarely in mind.

First, our children, after reaching the age of accountability, are free moral agents. We can teach, set limits, discipline, and love them before God. But in the end, our children will make their own choices, including the choice of whether to become involved sexually. We can't make that choice for them, and we're not responsible for it. Our children are. Therefore, don't take all the blame on yourself when your child makes wrong choices.

Second, this is a practical text and a book of hope. No, being a parent isn't easy—it never has been. But I sincerely believe that regardless of how good or bad a parent we feel we've been in the past, we can help our children make the right choices in the area of sexual involvement. And from my own experience I believe that parenting—even of a teenager in to-day's world—is a great, joyful experience.

Third, the most important message you can get from this book is that it is the relationship we have with our children which is most vital. Rules, teaching, guidelines, examples, and discipline are all significant. But none is as important as building a loving, accepting relationship with our children. It was the apostle Peter who, referring to the book of Proverbs, said, "Love will cover a multitude of sins" (1 Peter 4:8). Above all, we need to love our children and let them know we do.

Parenting can be tremendously rewarding. We *can* help our children resist the pressures to get involved in premarital sex. I'm convinced that we parents *can* make a difference.

Part I

♂ ———————————————————————————— ♂

Discovering
the
Root Causes

The most important thing to adolescents isn't knowledge or doctrine or even possessions. It's relationships. Young people need to feel accepted by someone, to feel they belong somewhere. And if they get more of that feeling from their peers than they do from their parents, it shouldn't be surprising that their peers exert more influence over them.

2 ♂

Understand Your Child

IF YOU THINK IT'S TOUGH being a parent today, try being an adolescent! Most of us would like to recapture some of our lost youth, but we would face a different world than what we grew up in if we could actually do that. Kids who grow up today have a much tougher time of it than you and I did. They face far more pressure and temptation. It's been said that a child today faces more sexual signals and temptations on the way to school that his grandfather did on Saturday night when he went out looking for them!

You may have trouble sometimes understanding or communicating with your child, and he or she may seem to be part of an entirely different world, but it's essential you remember that it's not easy to be a moral, Christian adolescent these days.

Even if you don't always get along with your child, and even if his or her peer group seems to have more influence than you do, your child wants your input, wants to be taught by you, wants to be able to look up to you. This includes the area of sexuality.

A 1983 study of churched families by Search Institute found this: among adolescents as a whole, the overwhelming preference for someone to whom they would most like to turn for help and advice with questions about sex was their parents. This was especially true of younger adolescents, but even as late as ninth grade, a majority preferred their parents' help and advice to that of friends or other adults.

With those thoughts as background, let's look at some facts about our children that are making it difficult for them to say no to the pressures toward premarital sex.

Raging Hormones

The adolescent years bring the onset of puberty, the time when a young person becomes sexually mature. Not only does the child become physically able to engage in sexual activity and reproduce at puberty, but the flood of sexual hormones is intense and continues to build through the early twenties.

This is a period of great confusion, curiosity, fear, and excitement. Everything in the young person's body is gearing up for sexual activity, and desire is great. Further, a person's body cannot tell if he or she is married or not, if sexual involvement is proper or not. All the young person's body tells him or her is that the desire is there, and that it's powerful.

It is a biological fact that puberty is arriving earlier all the time. One hundred years ago the average age of puberty was about sixteen. Just forty years ago, the onset of puberty was normally around age fourteen. But today, it's closer to twelve, which means those great physical changes and their attendant feelings hit when kids are younger and less mature emotionally than has been the case in the past. It also means that even if young people today were to marry at the same ages as in the past, they still have several more years during which they have to keep their feelings and desires under control.

Children are also maturing intellectually sooner than their parents did. Human knowledge has exploded in the last few decades, and our children are more informed as a result. But although they mature physically and intellectually earlier today, they are, on the average, far behind where their parents were emotionally. They are therefore less able to deal with the pressures they have to face.

There are a couple of reasons for this late emotional development. First, young people just don't have as much contact with adults in their families as they used to, and those adults are an important part of the emotional nurture of children. Whereas adolescents used to have a lot of contact with grandmothers and grandfathers, aunts and uncles—it wasn't that long ago that three or more generations of a family typically lived in the same house—today's mobile society often finds grandparents and other members of the extended family living hundreds and even thousands of miles away.

Adult contact is also limited by the busyness of the modern American family. With all the activities of parents and children—lessons and meetings and practices and games—it's difficult for the typical family to have meals together, much less significant discussions or even just plain fun as a family.

Interaction between parents and children is limited even further by the still-growing phenomenon of both parents working outside the home. This means more and more school-age children are coming home to empty houses—the "latchkey kids." Rather than interacting with a parent during the after-school hours, these youngsters have television or friends for companions. Fifty years ago, the average child had three to four hours a day of interaction with parents or extended family members. Today's child has only about fifteen minutes of interaction with parents a day. And twelve of those minutes are in a setting of critique, instruction, or criticism.

A second reason for the emotional immaturity of today's children is the instability and insecurity of family relationships. Virtually every child now in school knows someone whose parents are divorced—if his or her own aren't also. And as soon as children hear of a new separation which has taken place, their fear that the same thing will happen to *their* family is turned up another notch. Your own child has almost certainly felt this fear, whether or not it's been verbalized.

It seems that most of what they see happening around them today builds insecurity, not confidence, about the long-term viability of the family.

Putting this all together, we see that the human adolescent is a sex machine (biologically speaking), that the age of puberty is arriving earlier than ever, and that children today are less ready than ever from an emotional standpoint to handle their hormones in a mature, morally responsible way.

Expanding Adolescence

While earlier puberty is expanding adolescence downward, social and economic pressure is forcing it upward. More and more young people are choosing to delay marriage until they're well into their twenties and even thirties. This expanding adolescence increases the time between the onset of sexual maturity and the legitimate outlet for sexual activity in marriage. This puts enormous pressure on young people to indulge in premarital sex.

Although there are many reasons why an individual might choose to delay marriage, too often it is for selfish economic concerns. Many of today's young people want to get ahead in their careers and in their accumulation of status-conveying possessions as quickly as possible. That's a lot easier to do if you're free to work long hours without keeping a spouse waiting—and if you don't have the time and monetary responsibilities of parenthood.

Of course, there are times when economic considerations force a couple to postpone marriage, and I don't mean to fault them. But many other young people who could marry are choosing not to so that they can more easily pursue the BMW and the corner office.

My main point here is that while nature is expanding adolescence in one direction, human volition is simultaneously stretching it in the other. One hundred years ago a person's sexual awakening usually occurred within a year or two of marriage. There was little time when a person would even be tempted to become sexually active outside marriage. Today, however, it is not uncommon for more than a dozen years to pass between the onset of puberty and the time when a person marries. And those years are the time of greatest sexual desire. This puts tremendous pressure on a young person not to wait for marriage.

Children are also getting more information about sex at an earlier age than ever before. More and more, detailed information about sex is conveyed in movies, music, television, advertising, books, and magazines—and every other medium. We'll look at this in detail in the next chapter.

Just as one example, however, there are simply far more magazines with explicit sexual content than there used to be. When I was a teen, *Playboy* was considered racy, and it was about the only magazine of its type. Today, however, *Playboy* is thought to be tame compared to the many other magazines that are readily available.

Sex education classes in the schools are also distributing more and more information, and to younger children than in the past. This is partly out of concern over the epidemic of sexually transmitted diseases, and partly because of the equally serious problem of teenage pregnancy.

Further, just as the onset of puberty is coming at ever earlier ages, so also kids are becoming sexually active at increasingly younger ages. It's not uncommon any more for *preteens* to have sex on a regular basis. In fact, 50 percent of today's sexually active teen males had their first sexual experience between the ages of eleven and thirteen. Naturally, these immature kids are talking to their friends.

When adolescents—and even younger children—learn about sex in these ways, they're getting a biological education (which may or may not be accurate), but they're not being trained in moral responsibility. The media, their friends, and even their teachers are telling children how the body works; but they aren't telling young people how to handle their desires in a way that keeps them pure and honors God.

Moreover, children are learning the mechanics and physical aspects of sex, but for the most part they are not learning about the relational aspects of sex. It is not possible to teach sex apart from teaching character, because sex involves other people. Sex has to do with how you treat people. This is why we parents must develop and model healthy relationships before our children and both show them and explain to them the importance of relationships.

Peer Pressure

Peer pressure can be either negative or positive. But often today, peer pressure strongly encourages adolescents to become sexually involved. A recent poll conducted by the Louis Harris organization found that for both teenage boys and girls, social—or peer—pressure is the number one reason for premarital sex. (For girls, pressure from boys was the number two reason behind pressure from their own female friends.) The desire to be accepted and admired by peers is great, even if that acceptance comes at a high price.

To see just how this pressure works, consider these words from a high school girl: "The girls . . . start to view virginity as an embarrassment. Friends tease and pressure to the point of humiliating the virgin girl for not having sex with the opposite sex. Peers call them prudes or nerds or even go so far as to call them homosexuals because of their refusals to have premarital sex. Some will give in just to prove that they are just as normal as the next person."

Teens often respond to peer pressure because they get from their peers what they should be getting at home. Their friends will listen to them. They feel an acceptance among their peers. It is usually a conditional acceptance, but the rules are very clear as to what one needs to do to earn that acceptance. And their peers give our children an opportunity to develop relationships.

Now, there has always been peer pressure. But that force is far greater today than ever before because of instability and insecurity in the American family. If young people are unsure of their family relationships, they'll try all the harder to make other relationships secure—no matter what the price.

Two Cultures in Every Home

Finally, parents who are about forty years old or older may have two extremely different cultures with very different values living in their homes. There has always been a "generation gap" between parents and children. But until recently that generation gap existed with both parents and children at least having the same set of moral presuppositions. But now, the old world in which you and I grew up has passed and our adolescent children are living in a new one with a different set of rules, a new set of presuppositions. Yet we tend not to see it, especially when we interact daily with our children.

For most of the history of our nation, our society and its values were Judeo-Christian. Even those who weren't themselves Jews or Christians recognized the validity of laws and social values based upon the Bible. Thus, when a pastor or a parent told young people to abstain from premarital sex because it's a sin and is therefore wrong, the majority agreed. The culture as a whole would support those convictions. That's not to say, of course, that adolescents (and others) never engaged in premarital sex. But when they did, they knew it was wrong, and society even passed laws against it.

Since the late 1960s, however, we've been living in a different culture, a post-Christian society. The very basis of our society—its rules and mores—has changed. The sexual revolution has engulfed the nation. The validity of laws and values based on the Bible is no longer acknowledged by the majority. Instead, what adolescents hear from every corner of society is that what's right and wrong depends on the situation and the people involved; that if it feels good, you should go ahead and do it; that "love" doesn't restrain itself for the long-term good of the relationship but rather that "love" equals instant sexual gratification.

Teenagers have inherited a world which demands instant satisfaction—a world in which the events of an entire day warrant only 30 minutes of news, 300 years of history fit into a one-week miniseries, and food is tossed in the car window as

we drive by a restaurant. It is a world in which pocket calcula-
tors free us from having to think, videotapes rescue us from
having to read, and abortionists release us from taking responsibility. It is a world in which we can "have it all."

Many parents who left adolescence behind before 1968
simply don't realize the profound change that's taken place in
our culture. That's why they come up to me after a seminar
and say, "My parents and pastor told me not to do it, that it's a
sin, and that was good enough for me. I turned out all right.
That ought to be good enough for my kid." I try to explain that
the media, peers, music, public schools, and every other part of
society are telling their children just the opposite.

As you read through chapter 4, for instance, many of the
reasons adolescents say yes to sex will not make as much sense
if a teen is strongly committed to and understands the Christian faith and how to think Christianly—and is surrounded by
a support group of similar teens. But the reasons given make a
whole lot of sense for a teen who is committed to and lives by
the post-Christian ethic in which there are no absolutes except
that of "love" (whatever this may mean at the moment). And
most teens today, whether in public schools or Christian ones,
are surrounded by friends who understand only the post-
Christian ethic.

To overcome this culture gap with our children, we need
to first realize it exists. Then we need to give our children a lot
more information, and much sooner, than used to be necessary. Our children also need to know that this gap exists and
what the difference is between the two cultures. If we are going
to shape what our children think about sexuality rather than
letting our non-Christian culture shape it, we have to start
teaching the child before the values of society begin to mold
his or her understanding.

In this chapter, we've looked at some of the pressures our
children face every day. Next, we'll look more closely at this
post-Christian culture in which we now live and which is constantly tempting our children to say yes to premarital sex.

3 ♂

Understand Your Society

A COVER STORY DISCUSSING the communication between teens and their parents about sex recently appeared in *People* magazine. Not surprisingly, the magazine's poll found that teens aren't nearly as candid with their parents as their parents think they are!

What I found especially interesting, however, was that this issue of the magazine was stuffed full of pictures of beautiful young women in provocative poses wearing sexy clothing and not much of it. Some of these pictures were featured in the editorial content of the magazine, women it was featuring in stories. Others were in advertisements. Flipping through the pages gave the impression of one enticing image after another.

Now I don't mean to single out *People* and suggest it's worse in this regard than most other magazines. Unfortunately, what I saw there is so common in consumer magazines today that we hardly even notice it any more. This says something about both the mass media and our society as as whole.

The inescapable fact is that both the media and our entire society are saturated with sex. The result is that our children are constantly bombarded with highly charged sexual messages encouraging promiscuity.

The Influence of the Media

It should be obvious that the mass media have enormous influence. They greatly influence how we view the world, how we think and talk, what we wear and drive, what we consider to be important and unimportant, what's "hot" and what's not—virtually every aspect of life.

One of the most powerful tools of the media is television. Even if the producers and advertisers who are responsible for television's content weren't extremely effective communicators—which, in fact, they are—just the amount of time Americans spend watching TV would make it very influential. According to the A. C. Nielsen Company, the television ratings agency, the average American home has a television set turned on seven hours a day. That's almost fifty hours a week! And the average adolescent aged twelve to seventeen watches twenty-three hours of television each week!

Computer programmers have a phrase that's very applicable here: "Garbage in, garbage out" (GIGO). The Bible says something similar in Proverbs 23:7: "For as he thinks in his heart, so is he." What both these phrases suggest is that what you get out of something, whether it's a computer or a person, is basically what's been put in. In other words, what we and our kids fill our minds with pretty much determines what comes out in our thoughts, attitudes, words, and actions.

Thus, just because of the amount of time our children spend in front of the television, it has great impact in their lives, helping to shape them into the people they are and will become.

Of course, television isn't the only mass medium that influences our kids. Adolescents are the major audience for the movie industry, which is why the content and music in so many of today's films are aimed straight at them. And a typical weekend date for teens includes dinner at a fast-food restaurant followed by a movie.

With today's technology, the influence of movies extends even beyond the theater. The videocassette recorder brings ilms and their messages right into our homes. And when it omes to the subject of sex, the message most movies present is ven stronger and more explicit than that of television.

Music, especially rock music, is another powerful influnce on our young people. Adolescents today seemingly can't ive without having the radio or stereo on (if the television sn't), and that radio or stereo is usually playing rock at a vindow-shaking level. Rock musicians have become role mod-ls, and the message of their songs is bought wholesale by milions of children. Again, just the fact that young people are xposed to rock so much guarantees that this music will have a uge impact. And when the music is combined with visual mages in music videos, the effect is multiplied.

Although modern adolescents don't read as much as preious generations, books and magazines are still widely read nd extremely influential. This ranges from textbooks to ronance novels, from popular magazines like *Cosmopolitan* and *People* to pornography. In the overwhelming majority of these rinted materials, a clear message about sexuality is being onveyed, and you can be sure our kids aren't missing it.

Advertising is yet another enormous influence. And gain, even if it weren't practiced by skillful communicators, it vould still make a huge impact simply because we and our hildren are exposed to so much of it. The National Associaion of Broadcasters says the average household sees between eventy and ninety television commercials *per day.* As if this veren't enough, we have to add to that number all the radio ommercials, magazine and newspaper ads, and billboards to vhich we're daily exposed.

The Message of the Media

Just what are the media telling us about sex? The message hat comes through clearly is that if it feels good, do it; only rudes and the undesirable wait for marriage; do it as often as ou like and with as many different people as you like; there re no negative consequences to premarital sex; and once you marry, you can still sleep around—after all, almost everybod else is doing it!

During a year of average television viewing, a person te years old or older is exposed to more than 9,000 scenes o suggested sexual intercourse, sexual comments, or sexual innu endo. And of those scenes, more than 7,000, or about *80 per cent, portray sex outside* of marriage. That's what one averag adolescent sees in a year, year after year. By the age of twenty one has seen 90,000 sexual comments or suggested acts of se on television.

On TV soap operas, which have many adolescent fan (primarily girls, but also boys), the message is even stronger There, *94 percent* of the sexual encounters portrayed are be tween people not married to each other. Wrote one social com mentator, "On daytime soaps, gorgeous men and women ho in and out of bed like fleas in heat."*

In movies even more than television, the spurious idea i promoted that love equals sex—that is, as soon as a man and woman realize they're in love or even just "crazy about eacl other," the appropriate and reasonable next step is for them t jump into bed together. Movie after movie shows this to b normal behavior. And after young people see this pictured few dozen times, along with all the reinforcement the messag gets, they easily and even unconsciously begin to believe it.

Chicago film critic Roger Ebert sums up the movie indus try's approach to morality very well: "Media input is part o life . . . . Film contributes and film reflects. Yet it's a rar movie that deals with any kind of moral issue in a moral way."

Turning to books and magazines, the message of pornog raphy, whether it's soft-core like *Playboy* or more hard-core, i obvious. What's more revealing (no pun intended) is the way promiscuous messages about sex now permeate the more re spectable books and magazines.

Novels today typically carry at least one explicit se

---

* Lesley Jane Nonkin, *I Wish My Parents Understood* (New York Penguin, 1985) 149.

scene, usually between unmarried people. It almost seems the writers and editors consider it a requirement. Of course, romance is a part of life and so, properly, has always been an ingredient in fiction. But in the past, writers generally only suggested the sexual aspect of a relationship and left most of the encounter to the reader's imagination. Today, on the other hand, the sexual expression is described in minute and stimulating detail.

Another important difference is this: in the past, romance didn't imply that there would even be a premarital sexual relationship. Indeed, the idea of romance was that it would lead to marriage. And when there was a premarital relationship, all the characters would recognize that it was immoral. Today, on the other hand, books fuel the idea that going to bed together is the normal and perfectly acceptable thing for people who "love" each other to do.

The same message comes from our popular magazines, which apparently want to help us "do it" more enjoyably. Fashion magazines at the grocery store checkout feature articles like "How to Seduce a Man," "What to Do When Your Best Friend Makes Love with Your Boyfriend," and "Sinfully Sexy—Fourteen Red-Hot Men."

This same message also comes through loud and clear in advertising. The premise, of course, is that sex sells products. But in addition to selling products, ads also sell a perspective on sex, the perspective promoted by all the other media. They also feed society's preoccupation with sex, filling our eyes and minds with one beautiful, young, scantily clad woman after another.

The Permissiveness of Society

No doubt you've heard the conundrum about which came first, the chicken or the egg. Well, the same sort of uncertainty exists about whether the media merely reflect the society of which they are a part or are actively helping to shape it.

While the media have contributed to our moral decay, the

media certainly are not entirely responsible for what our society has become, and they are not the only forces affecting your child's view of sexuality. Our culture as a whole has adopted a promiscuous attitude toward sex, and this attitude confronts our children at every turn.

This mind set arises out of a fundamental change in the basis of morality. Formerly, most people's concept of morality was derived from an external standard—what God said in Scripture. But in our post-Christian society, most people's concept of morality is based on their own feelings and opinions. Morality is individual. This opens the door to a morality without standards.

Just how much our society has changed from basically moral to permissive (from a Judeo-Christian society to a post-Christian) is easily shown. In 1969, a Gallup poll found that 68 percent of all adults, and even 49 percent of young adults, felt premarital sex was wrong. In 1985, however—less than twenty years later—a Roper survey for *U.S. News & World Report* found that attitudes had completely changed. Now, 61 percent of all adults think premarital sex is acceptable, and 78 percent of young adults (ages 18–29) endorse that view.

Further, recent surveys have indicated that 65 percent of teen boys and 54 percent of teen girls want *more* sexual freedom in the future. And although 90 percent of teens say they believe in marriage, 74 percent of them say they would live with someone before or instead of marriage.

The sexual revolution of the late 1960s and 1970s has been well documented. The change in society's perspective has been so complete and so pervasive that a permissive attitude is taken for granted now by many parents as well as by their children. Thus, our children face overwhelming temptation and tremendous pressure from every direction.

Sex in the Proper Context

In a book like this, where I'm trying to deal with a problem that's threatening our families and society by seducing our

ildren, it's easy to leave a negative impression about sex
nerally. Let me make it clear that I am *not* against sex at all.

On the contrary, sex is a fabulous, wonderful gift from
od. He made us as sexual beings, and He declared all of
is creation to be good. Further, He made it so that we can
joy sex as well as reproduce by it. And we certainly ought
enjoy it.

However, having said this, it has to be added that God
signed sex to be part of a loving marriage relationship only.
ithin the love, lifetime commitment, and security of that
ntext, sex is God's gift to be enjoyed with His blessing. And
hen that gift is abused, outside the bonds of marriage, it
comes wrong.

We've now seen many of the pressures that are being put
pon our children daily to engage in premarital sex. With this
nderstanding, we'll be able to appreciate what the teens them-
lves say in the next chapter about why they choose to engage
sex.

For an in-depth look at the sexual influences on teens
day, see *Why Wait?* (pp. 15-70).

4 ♂

Why Youth Say Yes to Sex

THERE HAS ALWAYS BEEN PRESSURE on teens to have sex. Adam may not have told Eve, "If you love me, you'll go to bed with me," but I'm sure it did not take long for someone to think up that line. Today such lines are more effective than ever because young people are starved for relationships. They are crying out for love. Listen to the words of one young person:

When I was only fourteen years of age, I dated an eighteen-year-old boy. After a month or so of dating, he told me that he loved me and had to "have me." He said that if I loved him, I would have sex with him. And if I wouldn't, he couldn't control his desire for me and would have to break up with me.

What did I think at fourteen years of age? I knew sex was wrong before marriage, and I didn't want to lose my virginity. And yet I so desired to have a man love me. . . . So I finally gave in.

I felt so guilty afterwards. I can remember sobbing in my bed at night after I'd come home from being with my boyfriend. I wanted so much to have my virginity back. And yet it was gone, forever. My self-esteem certainly didn't improve, but worsened, and I needed my boyfriend's love more than ever. I began to feel so lonely inside, and yet there was no one I could turn to. Certainly not my father, who would really "hate" me if he ever knew what an awful thing I had done.

Well, after two years, I broke up with my boyfriend, but soon

had another, and went through the same cycle with him. And the
with another. Was I any more secure with myself? No, I was
puppet in any man's hands, for I wanted so desperately to fin
someone who would love me unconditionally.

Isn't that ironic? The very thing I searched for—unconditiona
love—was being offered to me conditionally. "If you love me, you'
do it."

I'm 27 now, and about six months ago I wrote in my journal t
the Lord these very words: "I felt lonely tonight. And I though
about the many times in my life that I have felt loneliness, intens
loneliness. As though I were here in life all alone. And I realized tha
what I was lonely for was a 'daddy.' To be able to call him up when
hurt and hear him say he understands and to listen to me. But,
never had that with my dad. And so I am lonely without that link t
my past.

"And then I thought about the young girl who this very nigh
will lose her virginity because she is searching for love—her daddy
love. And I wanted to be able to stop her somehow and tell her tha
she'll never find it in another man. How my heart is wrenched whe
I think of this girl . . . when I think of myself, so many years ag
And my life has been a search for my daddy's love. And in Jesus,
am found and I am loved. Forever."

So what do I want parents to know about their child's sexual
ity? Their sexuality is directly related to how they think of them
selves. If they don't find the love that they need at home, they'll g
looking for it elsewhere, but it will always be a cheap substitute fc
what a real daddy's love could be. . . .

Have you given your little girl her daddy's love? If you haven'
please do. Go to her, and tell her that you love her. And that she i
the most precious girl in the world to you. And what if you think it
too late? It's never too late. Even at 27, it wouldn't be too late.

This was written by one of those who entered the "Writ
Your Heart Out" essay contest conducted by the "Why Wait?
project. More than 1,000 essays were submitted, and man
wrote about "Why do people in your age group become sexu
ally involved?" "In Search of My Father's Love" is one of th
most poignant. I was surprised at the large number of reason
given for people becoming involved in premarital sex. Here ar

ome of the more prevalent ones, usually as described by the
eens themselves.

It Feels Good

This should come as no surprise. God made intercourse
feel good. A person who has premarital sex may feel guilt,
remorse, shame, or even hatred of the other person, but physically—and frequently relationally—premarital sex feels good.

"Where I live," one teen said, "many of my girlfriends
and guy friends are involved in sex because they just want to
do it. When I ask them why, they usually say it makes them feel
good, although some say they do it because their friends are
doing it."

God has given each of us a desire for intimacy and we feel
pain when that desire is not met. Developing relationships and
true intimacy is sometimes difficult and always takes time.
The easier and more predictable solution is to ease the pain
artificially. Just as pills can deaden real physical pain, sensory
feelings can deaden emotional pain. And for many, sex is the
drug that momentarily delivers them from emotional empti-
ness. It feels good. The letdown, the deepening pain, the fear,
the uncertainty will all come later, but for now, it feels good.
And so people become involved in premarital sex (or extramarital—it's not just teens who try to deaden pain this way).

Pressure from Boyfriend or Girlfriend

"Shauna and Bryan, her boyfriend," one teen wrote, "were
on a date to the movies. On the way home, Bryan drove them to
a dark secluded area where most couples went to park. Bryan
turned to Shauna and looked at her with very serious, but loving, eyes and asked her, 'Shauna, do you love me?' Shauna
chuckled and said, 'That's a dumb question. Of course, I love
you!' Bryan then said, 'If you love me you'll prove it by having
sex with me. If you won't then I will no longer be able to be your
boyfriend.' What could Shauna do? She would never want to

give up Bryan, but she knew sex before marriage was wrong. She decided she loved Bryan more and gave in. Within a week Bryan and Shauna had broken up and neither had respect for the other. Did Shauna really love Bryan? Not really, but she thought she did. However, that fear of losing Bryan overcame her."

Some teens have sex because they are afraid of losing a boyfriend or girlfriend. If a boy threatens to dump a girl because she won't give in, she may be fully aware that she is being manipulated, yet if she has become dependent on him emotionally, she will do what he wants.

I've Done It Once, Why Not Again?

Adolescents sometimes believe that once they've participated in sexual activity, there's no use in stopping. They feel they have already messed up and there's no way to change that. One girl said that she felt God could not use her because she wasn't a virgin and so she might as well have sex again.

A Christian who is sexually active before marriage and falls into this way of thinking has given up on God's forgiveness. But the beauty of God's forgiveness is that it is never-ending. We can come to Him in repentance at any time, for any reason, no matter how long we have been straying from Him.

A Lack of Understanding about Real Love

The biblical picture of love is one of giving without expecting anything in return, of accepting without conditions, and of security in a relationship without performance.

Children can grow up desiring to love their parents, but not feel secure in their relationship with them. When this happens, they often feel they have to perform in order to earn their parents' love. They are afraid their momentary shortcoming will lead to rejection. This can happen with well-meaning children trying to please Mom and Dad, but it has a stifling effect

Such children who have a lack of understanding about real love enter their teenage years equating love and performance. When they say, "If you love me, you'll have sex with me," they are only repeating their own distorted definition of love.

A lack of understanding about real love usually results in confusion about sex and love. Granted, they should go together in the right context, but they are not synonymous. They are two separate concepts. Sex is an act performed by two people committed to loving each other for life, while love, in varying degrees, can be felt by anyone. Love is not an act; love is a commitment.

Peer Pressure

What do teens say about peer pressure? Listen as several young people share what they feel:

"My three closest friends were all sexually active, or at least said they were, from our sophomore year on. It seemed as if they always got the girls, even though all they would talk about was using them, and how they 'got a piece last night.'"

"My parents are always telling me what to do and what not to do. I hate their nagging. Besides, everyone has done it. Nobody's a virgin."

"The peer pressure by friends is probably the hardest to face as a virgin, because people will tease. 'It's fun, you're missing out. Are you chicken or something? It's great. You won't get pregnant.'"

Peer pressure as it operates among today's teens sometimes becomes a kind of "moral blackmail." The basis for this blackmail is the group's power to accept or reject. And in our permissive society, sexual activity is often seen as an important criteria for admittance into a desired group. Even Christian teens, who have grown up with biblical morality, find themselves discarding or ignoring those values because of their fear of rejection.

The single most effective deterrent to negative peer pressure is a good self-image. The secure teen is the only one most likely to withstand peer pressure. Therefore, we need to teach our young people to see themselves as God sees them—with infinite worth and value because of God's creative/redemptive plan. Young people who find their acceptance in a loving/accepting relationship with God and their parents are better protected against moral blackmail from their peers. And such relationships should start with their parents.

Remember, if our kids can't talk to us, they will talk to their peers. If we don't spend time with them, they will spend more time with their peers. If they don't have intimacy at home, they will seek it among their peers. If they don't get hugs from dad, they will get hugs from their peers. If we won't listen to them, their peers will. Teens respond to relationships. That is why they are so responsive to their peers.

Rebellion

Jessica liked to be around her friends because when they were together, she didn't have to think about all the hurt her mom had caused her. One night Jessica had a party at her house. She met Joe, a cute, intelligent guy, and was immediately attracted to him. They talked a lot and got to know each other over the course of the evening. Nearly everyone at the party was paired off in different parts of the house. Jessica led Joe into her parents' bedroom and they had sex that night in her parents' bed. It was the ultimate way Jessica could think of to rebel against her mother and the hurt she had caused.

Rebellion is a form of reaction generally caused by a lack of relationship. Counselors say again and again how the "rebellious child" is often reacting to poor relationships, both between the parents and child and between the parents themselves.

When parents have a rebellious child on their hands, there are some initial steps they can take to reestablish the relationship. The initial reaction of many parents is to impose more rules on the young person. But this seldom works, if a relationship has not been established with the one making the rules.

The teenager will rebel against authority since he is not convinced the authority figure has his best interest in mind. A battle results, with parents and children pitted against each other rather than working together toward an understanding. What should a parent do with a rebellious child?

First, back off on as many rules as possible. Don't simply resort to "grounding." Let your child know you want to rebuild the mutual trust you need. You are still in charge, but one can't show his children he trusts them if they have no opportunity to prove themselves trustworthy. Exercise caution, however, because a radical change will cause confusion.

Next, focus on your children and listen to them. You have to know what is going on in their heads. Listening to your teenager lets him know he is important to you. As you and your teenager become more important to each other, you will want to spend more time together. As the relationship and trust are gradually reestablished, the rebellion will become less of an issue.

Curiosity

One of the main reasons teens experiment with sex is curiosity. Most of the thousands of messages we receive each year about sex portray it as something exhilarating. No wonder teenagers wonder, *What does it feel like? Is it really as great as they say?* People have a natural curiosity about the unknown, and if teenagers learned about the facts of sex from their parents, they wouldn't have to do their own research.

Parents, therefore, should assume the responsibility of educating their kids about sex and regulating what they are exposed to. This doesn't mean children should be sheltered, but it does mean there needs to be open, frank discussion about the sexual messages and images adolescents receive so that their curiosity will be satisfied by their parents.

One of the ways this curiosity can be satisfied is to let young people know their parents enjoy sex. It would be difficult for parents who have rarely or never discussed sex to suddenly be candid with their teenagers, but it is possible. Such honesty and openness is better when started early. It will help take the mystique away from sex. The best way to make this fact clear to your children is to let them see you enjoying hugs and kisses with your mate and to verbalize that you enjoy being close to the child's mom or dad. It's therefore something they observe in the warmth and security of a committed marriage.

Our goal as parents is not to keep sex among teenagers unknown, just unexplored.

As an Expression of Love and a Response to the Need to Be Loved

A relationship. Acceptance. Security. Self-esteem. Knowing they are loved and can love others. Every teenager must have these needs met and we as parents play a vital role in meeting them for our children. Giving our children a relationship, acceptance, security, a healthy self-esteem, and letting them know that they are loved and can love others is far more important than giving them money, educational opportunities, a family reputation, or presents.

If they don't get love at home, they will seek it outside the home. One teenager explained it, "For instance, a girl's family is really having problems and she needs someone to listen to her, care about her, and most of all, love her. In her eyes, she needs someone who will just make her forget her problems, someone she can hold on to for security. She meets the 'perfect guy,' but really this guy is having basically the same problems and is looking for security as well. Neither one of them knows what real love is, and they may mistake it for sex. This is where a lot of people my age get into trouble."

As psychologist Rollo May pointed out, we use the body as a buffer to avoid psychological intimacy. It is much easier to jump in bed and share our bodies with someone than it is to share our innermost thoughts. And the excessive sexuality in our culture today is indicative of our inability to experience true intimacy. An adolescent who had been very much involved sexually with various men wrote, "It is far easier today to bare your bottom than to bare your soul."

Teens not only have a need to love, but to be loved. "It is obvious," one teen wrote, "that the emotion teenagers fear most is loneliness. The thought of being without love leads most teenagers to believe that sex leads to love."

Roger Simon's *Chicago Tribune* column, "Muffled Scream of Ruined Dreams," is a heartbreaking account of one woman's search for love:

"Takes two to tango, doesn't it?"

"Yes," she said, "But I was looking for love. That's all I was looking for."

Her name is Jane. She is in her 20s and floundering somewhere in the backwash of the sexual revolution.

"When I was 12, my mother told me about sex and how it wasn't right until marriage," she said. "My mother got married when she was 16 and had children right away. She had eight children and she let us know what getting pregnant and accepting responsibility was all about. She let us know it is not some easy thing."

If you read the surveys, kids are not supposed to even care any more about things like virginity and what Mom would think. But I have a feeling there are thousands of kids out there who care very much.

"So what happened?" I asked her.

"I fell in love," she said. "But I let the guy know I wasn't going to have sex with him. That was for marriage."

"And?"

"And he said, 'How am I going to marry you if we don't find out if we're compatible first?' That's what he said. Compatible."

"And you fell for that?"

"I liked him," she said. "I loved him. So I did it. And he liked it. And we got engaged. And then he dumped me."

"And you felt used."

"I felt hurt and used," she said. "I never should have done it. If I had held back, he would have respected me."

"So why did you do it?"

"You know how many women are out there?" she said. "And he was a good-looking guy. There were plenty of women who were willing. I did it because I wanted him to love me. And that was stupid of me. Making love doesn't make them love you."

"From now on, no sex until I get married," she said. "I'm not giving myself any more. I feel like what I've done is wrong. Before you can love someone else, you have to love yourself, you have to respect yourself. If I had respected myself, I would have remembered what my mom had told me."

Further resources: Why Wait? (pp. 71–186) and *Teens Speak Out.*

Part II

♂—————————————————————♂

Treating
the
Root Causes

If you remember nothing else from this book, please fix in your mind at least this one truth: Rules without relationship equal rebellion—either active resistance or passive indifference. If you really want to help your child say no to premarital sex, the most important thing for you to do is not to establish rules but to build a strong, loving relationship with your child.

5 ⚥

Parent + Child Relationship = Reduced Sexual Involvement

DANNY WAS A BRIGHT Christian teenager who had come to me for counseling. "Sometimes I feel so alone like no one cares. My folks live in their own world and I live in mine." He looked up and gazed past me as he spoke more slowly, "It didn't always seem to be that way . . . I know it sounds crazy, but I want them to leave me alone and yet, I want to be a part of their lives. Most of the time, they do leave me alone and it gets pretty lonely."

It is this sense of feeling alienated from family, a lack of relationship, that makes young people extremely susceptible to sexual involvement. Yet, I'm convinced it is not sex they are seeking.

If I were asked to give the number-one contributing factor to the adolescent sexuality crisis, at the top of my list would be adolescent alienation brought on by parent inattentiveness. If you want to insulate your child from the many sexual pressures, develop a close open relationship of mutual respect and love. Establishing sexual prohibitions and rules without a relationship often leads to rebellion. But, rules within the context of a loving parent relationship, generally lead to a positive response. The thesis is: as parents provide the proper emotional, spiritual and psychological stability for their child in a loving relationship, closeness will increase and temptation to seek intimacy through sexual involvement will decrease.

There are five elements that I would like to share which may help you develop a closer, healthier parent/child relationship. Applying these relational building blocks goes a long way toward avoiding adolescent alienation.

Provide Acceptance

A child needs to be convinced that no matter what happens, no matter what he or she does, our acceptance and love will never waver. This acceptance will give our children the sense of *security* which they so desperately need, especially in today's world.

Sometimes, parents offer performance-based (or conditional) acceptance. As long as children perform as their parents require, they will accept them. But if the children fail, the parents' love and acceptance is temporarily withdrawn.

One way to communicate unconditional acceptance is to praise *effort* more than *success*. The crucial question is not whether your child won a sporting event, or got an A in school or drew a standing ovation for a performance, but whether or not that was the best he or she could do.

My son, Sean, has developed into quite a soccer player and naturally I'm very proud of him. But my acceptance of and love for him does not depend on how well he plays soccer. I don't talk to him about how well he has done or how his success compares to someone else's. Instead, I determine whether he gave the game his best effort. I then reassure him that if he did his very best, that's all I'll ever ask of him, and that my love for and acceptance of him will never depend on how well he performs.

Suppose I were to get into the habit of taking Sean out for ice cream after games in which he plays well and gets several goals. And what if we *always go straight home after games in which he played hard but lost?* After a season of this habit, Sean would receive a message, loud and clear, that at least when it comes to soccer, Dad's acceptance of him depends on his playing well.

When I realized this could happen, I made a point of telling Sean, and of repeating it throughout the season, that I would accept him just as much if he didn't score a single goal all year. And when I praise him for his play, I talk more about his effort than I do about the number of goals he scored.

To make sure the point gets through, I'm careful to take him out for a treat after games his team loses at least as much as after those it wins.

Dottie and I are also careful in what we say about other people in front of our children. Children will often apply to themselves what they hear the parents say about others.

For example, suppose I take Sean to a major league baseball game, and at a crucial point, one of the home-team batters strikes out and ends an inning. Then suppose I start ripping that player up one side and down the other. "You bum!" I shout. "What kind of jerk are you? They ought to ship you back down to the minors!"

What message is Sean getting from my tirade? *The next time I miss a goal, Dad will think I'm a jerk, too.* Never mind whether it's logical for Sean to compare himself with a major league ballplayer; that's exactly what he'll think.

Sometimes I'm asked for my opinion of other people who have sinned or failed morally. If I'm too quick to denounce the people involved or condemn them for what they said or did, I'm sending a subconscious message to my children that if they ever do anything questionable, they better not tell me about it or I will condemn *them*, too.

That's not what I want my children to think and so I am very careful to say, "Kids, God hasn't called me to judge other people. They will answer to Him, not me, for whatever they have or haven't done. God calls me to try to heal the Body of Christ, not tear it apart." And the subconscious message I trust they get from such an answer is that if I don't reject others when they do wrong, I won't reject my children, either. This doesn't mean I don't denounce the sin. But it does mean that I still accept the individual as one created in the image of God and of infinite worth, even though I do not approve of the sin.

Give Appreciation

Expressing appreciation for who your child is gives him or her a sense of significance. Children need to know that their parents appreciate them for who they are. Yet many adolescents, especially the teenagers I talk to, feel that their parents are always finding fault with them, pointing out what they're doing wrong, admonishing them to clean up their rooms, wash the dishes, etc. Dottie and I make a conscious effort to find things our children do that is worthy of praise. We've had to work at making this a habit. Our motto has become, "Try to catch them doing something good."

To borrow a phrase from Mamie McCullough, be "a good-finder." Look for the good things your child is doing. And when you find something, be quick to express appreciation.

Be honest with your appreciation. People—especially children—can usually detect insincerity in a hurry. We shouldn't fake appreciation just because we feel we have to find something to praise. If we look closely, we should be able to find plenty of good things our children are saying and doing for which we can express genuine appreciation.

Be Available

When you as a parent make yourself available to your children it gives them a sense of importance and worth. Simply put, if you spend time with your children, they will feel important because they perceive themselves as a priority in your life. And a child yearns to know that this is the case.

Being available to your child will also bring special rewards to you in the future. As my wise wife, Dottie, says, "If we spend time with our kids now, they'll spend time with us later. If we show an interest in them now, they'll show an interest in us later."

I know that as parents we have many demands on our time and that the kids themselves are going in twenty different directions at once. It's largely out of this concern that the concept of "quality time" developed. The idea is that you don't have to spend a lot of time with your child (quantity) in order to be a good parent, as long as the time you do spend is "quality" time.

While I agree that we need to spend quality time with our children, I'm also convinced that there simply is no substitute for spending quantity time with our kids. Making ourselves available will communicate to them that they are important to us—a key ingredient to avoiding adolescent alienation.

Here are just a few ideas for making and spending time with children. Allow them to stay up an hour past their bedtime, and spend that time with them with no distractions. Take the phone off the hook. Talk, play games, wrestle on the floor, maybe watch a special on television, or whatever. The idea is that this is a special occasion, and they have your undivided attention.

Ask your teenager to go with you when you need to run errands, and leave the radio off. This is a good time to talk, and it's also an opportunity for you to model the kinds of attitudes and behavior you want to develop in your teenager.

If your child is small, get a magnifying glass, and go around the backyard together, looking at bugs and plants through it. When you go to the beach, look at sand crabs through it. How about going for a walk around the block together—backwards! Your neighbors will think you're crazy, but so what? You'll have a ball.

You're familiar with the idea of progressive dinners, where you go to a different house for each course of a meal. But how about a progressive dinner with your child at different fast-food restaurants? Or try going to a shopping mall together, sitting on a bench in a busy area, and watching the shoppers go by. Pick out the funniest people, the happiest, the saddest, the weirdest-dressed, the best-dressed, and so on. Not only does this provide conversation, but it will also give you a tremendous insight into your child's perspective—what he or she thinks is funny, happy, sad, or weird.

Availability also has another meaning besides spending planned time with our children. It means that they are more important than anything we may be doing when we're not with them, and so they are free to interrupt. If I'm writing in my study at home, for example, my kids know they are always welcome to come in and talk with me. I'll *gladly* set aside my work for a few minutes with them.

I had the importance of making people a priority over projects brought home for me a number of years ago. I've always been involved in writing books and scripting movies. When I would be writing, if my wife or my children would come in to talk to me, I'd always say, "No, I can't talk right now. Perhaps later." There were many times when my children really needed me, but I shunned them because of what I was involved in.

One day I finally realized that I will always have projects. I will always have deadlines from publishers. I will always have a crisis to deal with. I am that kind of person. But I won't always have a child coming in and wanting to ask me a question, who seeks my advice, just a hug, or needs to be comforted. And so I made a commitment before the Lord that by His strength I will never allow projects or things to become more important to me than people, especially my own family.

It hasn't been easy, but I try to develop the attitude that no matter what I am doing, if one of my children or my wife wants to talk to me, I set aside what I am doing, look them squarely in the eye, and listen to them and answer their question.

Availability. It's vital to our children because it gives them a sense of importance and worth. And there's just no substitute for it.

Show Affection

Showing affection to your children will give them a sense of *lovability*. That is, if a child feels confident that *Mom and*

Dad love me, then he or she is also able to think, *Other people will be able to love me, too.* And that confidence is essential to a child's self-esteem and ability to have good relationships outside the family.

Children can't get too much affection. They need lots of verbal love; they need to hear "I love you" over and over. I try to say it to each of my children at least four or five times a day, whether in person or on the telephone. They also need lots of physical love such as hugs, kisses, shoulder pats and rubs, and head strokes. Naturally, it's easier to do this with older children if you started when they were younger, but it's never too late to start. Children drink in affection like a desert soaks in rain.

Part of affection, too, is just having fun with your children. When they see you're having fun and are glad to be with them, it reassures them of your love. Not long ago, we were on vacation, and we had taken a friend of Kelly's, my oldest daughter, with us. One day while we were there, the two girls said they would like to have some fun styling my hair. I couldn't imagine it, but I figured, why not? However, I said I would go along with it only if they'd go out to dinner with me that night and sit with me.

They had a great time doing up my hair in a sort of a Mohawk. And that night we went out for dinner, but I had to wear dark glasses!

Let me emphasize again that you can't give children too much affection. Some will shrink back from physical affection and complain a little as they approach adolescence, but even then they basically eat it up, especially in private and particularly if you've already been giving it to them for years.

A study showed that 61 percent of mothers will give verbal affection each day to their five-year-olds. By the time a child is nine, only 37 percent of the mothers do it every day. For fathers, 40 percent express verbal affection to five-year-olds each day and only 24 percent do it to nine-year-olds. Physical affection is more common than verbal affection. Eighty-three percent of the mothers gave a hug or a kiss to their five-year-olds each day and 49 percent gave it to their nine-year-olds. Sixty-four percent of the fathers demonstrated physical affection to five-year-olds each day and 33 percent to nine-year-olds. It scares me to think how little affection children of fifteen are getting, when they actually need more. The trend to give less and less affection to our children needs to be reversed since we live in a very emotion-oriented society.

It's the affection you give children that will build in them lovability.

Establish Accountability

Establishing accountability into your relationship with your children will give them a sense of responsibility. I'm not talking here only about letting your children be responsible to you. That's only half the story. It is also good to make yourself accountable to your children.

I've asked my children to help me to be the best parent I can be by pointing out areas where I can improve. I also ask them to point out those times when I say or do things that are contrary to what I've tried to teach them.

Not long ago, we were all going out to a fast-food place for dinner. Everyone except Kelly wanted to go to the same place. And in her frustration she made some disparaging remarks about the place everyone else wanted to go. I corrected her for her attitude and language.

We compromised on the choice of restaurants by agreeing that those who wanted to go to the one place would be dropped off there, and Dottie and I would take Kelly to the place she liked. As we pulled up to the first restaurant, I said, "Everyone out for the gag bag."

As we pulled away, Kelly promptly and firmly pointed out to me that I had just done what I had reprimanded her for. She was right. I swallowed hard and thanked her for showing me my inconsistency. She not only helped me be a more responsible person, but I was also given the opportunity to set a proper example of how she should respond when called into account for her own attitudes and actions.

On another occasion, I once asked each of my children who was old enough, to write down five ways they wanted others to treat them. The number one thing they listed was kindness. Building on that and applying Matthew 7:12 (the Golden Rule) to it, I said that if they wanted others to treat them with kindness, they should start by being kind to others themselves. I pointed out that we needed to be especially kind to each other in the family.

Numerous times since then, when I've noticed one of my children being unkind to someone else, all I've had to say is, "Remember when we listed how we wanted others to treat us?" And that's been enough to make them aware of their attitudes and actions.

I've also tried to help my children understand the matter of accountability and how we treat others in terms of our relationship with God. One day I was in the car with Sean and we pulled into the parking lot of a busy shopping center. Somehow I found two empty spaces side by side near the entrance of the store where I wanted to shop.

When I first pulled in, I didn't do a very good job of it, taking up part of both empty spaces and making it impossible for anybody to park next to me. I was tempted to leave the car that way and go on in, but it occurred to me that this was not a loving thing to do and that it was also a good opportunity to teach Sean a lesson from 1 Corinthians 13:4–7.

I backed the car out and reparked properly, staying within the lines of one space. "Sean," I said, "do you know why I bothered to do that? If I took up both those parking places, someone else who wants to go to this store would have to park a long way away, and that wouldn't be very loving of me, would it?"

I've found that little lessons like this really stick in my children's minds, helping them see I'm accountable to God for how I treat others as well as how I treat them. It teaches them responsibility in the process.

The Building Blocks of a Relationship

Acceptance, appreciation, availability, affection, and accountability. Acceptance gives your child a sense of security. Appreciation gives him or her a sense of significance. Availability gives your child a sense of importance and worth. Affection builds a sense of lovability. And accountability gives a sense of responsibility. These five elements built into your own relationship with your child will make it a strong and healthy one. And let me say again that the relationship we have with our children is the most important key to helping him or her say no to sexual involvement. If our relationship is good, our children are far more likely to understand, respect, and obey our rules.

TRY IT YOURSELF
Ideas for Building a Healthy Parent-Child Relationship

This chapter has many ideas in it for creative ways in which you can build a healthy parent-child relationship. Here are six more.

1. Throughout the day as you think of things to tell your children, write them down in short notes: "You looked nice in your green sweater today." "Thanks for washing the car." "Let's go shopping for new tennis shoes tonight." Then begin leaving these notes at a designated place such as the kitchen counter, where the kids know to look for them each day.

2. Take your appointment book to the dinner table tonight. Show each of your family members the unassigned times in your schedule over the next two weeks, and write in their names at the times you agree upon. Then surprise them by turning to the following two weeks and doing the same thing again. Try a breakfast out on a Saturday or Sunday, a lunch out during your lunch break, or an hour before dinner on a day you leave work early. Let your child choose how the time will be spent.

3. Do you know your teen well? How easily can you answer these questions: What book is he or she reading now? Which is his or her favorite television program, entertainer, song? What are his or her teachers' names? Who is his or her best friend? What is your teen's greatest unfulfilled desire? What qualities do friends most

admire about your child? What does he or she enjoy most doing with you? (Have you done it recently?) What would your teen claim to be best at? For questions you can't answer easily, talk them over when you take your teenager out for breakfast next week.

4. Could you take one of your children with you on your next business trip? It might sound absurd at first, but what better way to spend quality time with the child, communicate how important he or she is to you, and help your child understand your job and the "real world" out there? Spell out the ground rules which will make the child's presence work with your trip objectives. If he or she will miss some school, take lessons along to fill up the time you'll be busy. Plan on some time to visit a historical site or take in some fun activity unique to your destination. One dad has the objective of taking each child with him once a year.

5. Plant a tree in honor of each of your children on his or her next birthday. It will not only give them something to care for, it will also provide a long-lasting reminder of their special day and an interesting perspective on their lives as both they and the trees grow older.

6. Praise your children's creativity by displaying whatever is the object of creativity or achievement. Try these ideas: a. Hang drawings on the wall at the places where most of their fingerprints are found. b. Make placemats by sealing artwork between two layers of clear contact paper. For changeable placemats, put drawings inside plastic folders. c. Arrange drawings on the dining table beneath a clear plastic tablecloth. d. Display art under the glass of your coffee table. e. On your living room wall, hang a frame with an easily removable back that can hold a different piece of art each month. f. Drawings you want to preserve permanently can be sprayed with hairspray as a fixative.

Further Resources: His Image—My Image and *Evidence for Joy.*

6 ☿

How to Model a Context for Sex

THE RELATIONSHIP WE HAVE with our children is their first line of defense in trying to help them say no to the pressures to engage in premarital sex. And right up there in importance with it is the relationship we have with each other as their mother and father. It takes a secure child to say no to pressure, and a great deal of that security comes from knowing that the relationship between Mom and Dad is secure.

Since that's true, one of the greatest things I can do for my kids is to love their mother. If kids don't have the confidence that Mom and Dad love each other and will always be together, they have to worry about the permanence of every relationship, including their own future marriages. And if you can't count on marriage to meet your human need for love and intimacy forever, why wait for marriage to enjoy sex?

It is significant that the verse we parents like to quote to our children—"Children, obey your parents in the Lord, for this is right" (Eph. 6:1) comes immediately after Ephesians 5:33 where Paul tells each husband to "so love his own wife as himself, and let the wife see that she respects her husband." A secure home that comes from a husband and wife loving each other and modeling love, obedience, and respect in responding to each other is one basis for obedience in the children. Ephesians 6:4 says, "Fathers, do not provoke your children to wrath,

but bring them up in the training and admonition of the Lord."
One way we can provoke our children to wrath is to fail to
provide a model for them of a family relationship in which the
father loves the mother.

The Search for Intimacy

I think it is a misnomer to say that we have had a sexual
revolution in the last twenty years. Instead, what we have had is
a revolution in the search for intimacy. Most young people who
get involved in premarital sex aren't really looking for sex per
se. They want intimacy—communication, dialogue, to know
and be known, to love and give love, to understand and to be
understood.

That intimacy used to be found in the family. Kids
received the love and security they needed from Mom and
Dad and brothers and sisters. Today, however, with the family
falling apart, such intimacy can no longer be found in many
homes. As a result, young people grow up with two great
fears: that they'll never be loved, and that they'll never be able
to truly love someone else.

We are all born with the need for and the capacity to love,
but this doesn't mean that effective loving comes automatically. On Valentine's Day several years ago, David Hartman
interviewed Dr. Salk, the family psychologist, on "Good Morning, America" and asked him two very profound questions.
First he asked, "Is everyone born with the capacity to love?"

Dr. Salk's simple answer was, "Yes."

Next Hartman asked, "Then why don't we have more love
in the world?"

That's a logical and simple question, isn't it? Yet it's very
profound. Why *isn't* there more love?

Dr. Salk responded wisely, "David, even though we are
born with the capacity to love, we need to learn *how* to love."
Then he turned to the camera and added, "The greatest thing
you parents can do for your children is to love each other."

Dr. Salk was absolutely right. There's the problem in a
nutshell. We learn to love from seeing our parents love each

other. We learn it as we see modeled the giving and receiving of love between Mom and Dad. *But so many children today are seeing exactly the opposite modeled in their families and in the families of their friends.* Too often the American home is no longer a place of warm intimacy and expression of love between a husband and wife.

One teenager wrote that an adolescent boy might rush into sex because "he is anxious to push this relationship into maturity in his search for intimacy. When they are making out, it gives him such a sense of security and he 'knows' that they are really starting to get close."

A single young adult wrote, "The reason I see as the most common for sex before marriage is the overwhelming need to be close to another human being, to make emotional contact, to keep from being lonely and to feel cared for."

Do you see what's happened? Kids need intimacy and love. They should be learning it and getting it at home, beginning with Mom and Dad's secure relationship. But when they can't find it there, they go looking elsewhere, often in a sexual involvement.

The Need for a Love Model

My wife Dottie has pointed out an important difference she realized when reading Ephesians 5:33: "Nevertheless let each one of you in particular so love his own wife as himself, and let the wife see that she respects her husband." The difference is that while the primary need of a woman is love, the primary need of a man is respect. Both men and women equally need love and respect, but it seems women desire a deep, loving relationship. Love motivates a woman and meets her deepest need. Men, on the other hand, seem to long to be respected as the provider and protector of the home. Thus, when I talk about showing love, I'm talking primarily to husbands. When I talk about showing respect, I'm talking primarily to wives.

Dottie says that for a man to feel respected by his wife, he needs to know that she supports him. She will stand behind him and admire him. She believes in him and will defend him. He needs the assurance she will encourage him, and that she is his greatest fan.

Fathers need to model love and mothers need to model respect to our children so that they will feel secure, have their intimacy needs met, and learn how to give and receive love and respect. But practically speaking, how do we model love and respect?

First, love and respect need to be verbalized. Children need to hear Mom and Dad tell each other, "I love you," or "I believe in you." Don't be shy about saying something like this to your spouse in front of your children—they need to hear it.

I frequently give verbal reassurance of my love and respect for my wife to my kids also. I'll say to them, "You know, your mother is the most fantastic woman in the world. I can't believe how lucky I am to be married to her! I sure do love her." When I call home during my travels and one of the children answers the phone, I'll ask, "How's that wonderful wife of mine doing?" And then I'll mention one specific thing about her that I really appreciate.

This verbalizing of love can come in a negative context as well. During our oldest child's preteen stage, there were times when my wife and daughter found themselves clashing in an occasional tug-of-war. And during this time, Kelly got into the habit of sassing her mother, usually while I was out of town.

Because Dottie was there every day and Kelly's sassing had gradually become more common, she didn't fully realize the disrespect Kelly was showing. Dottie therefore tolerated her behavior. One time, however, Kelly sassed Dottie while I was home, and I overheard it.

I sat Kelly down in a chair. Then I got down on one knee and looked her squarely in the eye. "Young lady," I said, "you might talk to your mother that way, but I'll never permit you to talk to my wife that way! I love that woman."

Believe it or not, that one stern message broke Kelly of the sassing habit. Just a few months ago, she started to sass Dottie in my presence again. Then all of a sudden she caught herself, turned to me, and said, "Oh, Daddy, I can't do that to your wife, can I?"

Another way I verbalize my love and respect for Dottie in front of our children is by leaving lots of little love messages for Dottie to find and the kids to see. Around Valentine's Day, stores have mushy cards and stickers and I'll buy a bunch of them to use all year long. Then before I leave on a trip, I'll hide these all over the house for her, and I'll often ask the kids to suggest where I should put them. They've left them on the milk jug in the refrigerator, on the shower door, in her bathrobe, on her pillow, in a dresser drawer—just about anywhere.

Dottie really enjoys these little reminders of my love, and the children have a blast watching her find them. And all that time, they're learning how to give and receive love.

Another suggestion is to involve your children in helping plan special events for your spouse. A few years ago, I got the idea of asking my kids to help me plan my anniversary celebration with Dottie. I got them together and said, "Now look, I'm going to take your Mom away for a couple of days up to Laguna Beach." They know that's just about our favorite place for a short vacation. "What can I do to really express to your mother that I love her?"

The children and I had a lot of fun planning that anniversary, and I've tried to make it a practice ever since to consult them for gift ideas, party ideas, and mini-vacation ideas for their mother.

To help me know better how to love my wife, not only have I asked her for insights on what shows her I love her, but I have asked many wives what communicates to them that their husbands love them. The list has not only been eye-opening for me, but it is quite long. I share it with you because it might give you a guide to loving your wife as it has me.

How My Husband Models Love

- He initiates family devotions.
- He initiates conversation on a deeper level.

- He gives me tasteful public displays of affection—winks, pats, eye contact.
- He verbalizes to the family that "my wife is a special person."
- He does something with me that I like to do that he doesn't like to do.
- He verbalizes his love for me to others by bragging on me.
- He is quick to forgive. He shows unconditional love and acceptance.
- He makes sure that I have time for myself and for the Lord.
- He holds me accountable.
- He gives me special surprises and gifts.
- He remembers special days.
- He listens with eye contact, silence, and remembers what I said.
- He values my feelings even if they are not rational or logical.
- He shares his feelings with me and demonstrates trust.
- He loves our children and notices the little things they do.
- He notices the way I look and dress.
- He compliments me on the special things and notices when I work hard at something.
- He helps me with routine tasks like cleaning off the table.
- He babies me when I am sick.
- He initiates and takes care of an entire date.
- He has love for and interest in my family.
- He is sensitive to my moods and, when I am down, encourages me and says something kind.
- He is disciplined and sets goals.

Here is a list for wives similar to the one above for husbands.

How My Wife Models Respect

- She verbally confirms trust in me.
- She honors, supports, and praises me in public and in front of our children.
- She makes time for me and offers her time to do my interests.
- She seeks my advice.
- She encourages me to be all I can be.
- She never criticizes me in public.
- She listens attentively.
- She believes in me and knows I will do the right thing.
- She trusts and supports my decisions.
- She verbalizes that she loves and respects me.
- She affirms me by suggesting that others seek me out for advice or counsel.
- She gives me freedom and respects my private time.
- She does not flirt with other men.
- She holds a high opinion of who I am, what I do, and what I say.
- She prepares my favorite meals.
- She allows me to dream and set goals and helps me to achieve those dreams.

Marriage: The Context for Sex

I mentioned earlier that my wife and I often display physical affection for each other in front of our children and that I'm convinced it's healthy. Taking that a step further, our children know that Dottie and I have sex together and that we really enjoy it. Of course we're modest and decent about it.

It's interesting that many children, even as adults, have trouble imagining that their parents enjoy God's gift of sex. It is a natural and beautiful part of the marriage relationship, and children need to know that. When they see Mom and Dad modeling affection in the proper context (the marriage relationship), they learn that this is the right place for it. They learn that sexual intimacy is a good thing. And they learn it's still possible to have a relationship that will satisfy all their needs and honor God, too, even in today's world.

The Single Parent

If you are a single parent, you don't need me to tell you that you face an especially tough job. Whether it's through death or divorce, you don't have a spouse with whom you can model a strong, loving relationship. If you're married but your relationship with your spouse is cold, at least you have hope that through love, work, counseling, and prayer, your marriage can become what it ought to be. The single parent, however, doesn't have that hope. What do you do?

Unfortunately, there is no easy answer. Other people can be brought into your child's life to help make up for the absence of a father or mother. In chapter 10, we will consider that in more detail. And as long as there is no threat of violence, abduction, or moral harm, it's best if both parents, even though divorced, stay active in a child's life.

Still, if you're a single parent, there's no way you can model a loving marriage relationship for your child. There are only three things I can suggest. *First,* even more than the married parent, you need to "overdose" your children with love. You need to spend time with them and be creative in planning activities and discussion. As much as possible, you should supply your child's need for parental love by yourself. I know it takes energy and enthusiasm, two things most single parents don't have much of because they live under greater-than-normal pressures due to work and household responsibilities, but it's what your child desperately needs. Aggressively loving your children takes a firm commitment on your part.

Second, even if you're divorced, you should talk to your child realistically but positively about what marriage *can* be. You can paint for your child a work picture of what married love is all about. You can instill the hope that a lasting, satisfying marriage is a very real possibility. Don't be afraid to admit any mistakes you might have made.

Finally, you should demonstrate by your actions as well as by your words that marriage is the only proper setting for a sexual relationship. In other words, as a single parent, you yourself have to resist all the pressures of our society to engage in premarital sex.

TRY IT YOURSELF
Ideas for Modeling a Solid Marriage Relationship

Modeling a solid marriage relationship takes constant work. Doing a lot of little things all the time is much more important than doing only a few occasionally. Here are some suggestions for those little activities.

1. Don't forget little expressions of love. A dandelion from among those stubborn weeds in the lawn, a compliment on appearance, a love note in the lunch box or attaché case, a peppermint on the pillow . . . they will all work wonders.

2. Remember the value of playfulness. Romance thrives on laughter and childlike pleasures like walking in the rain, skipping pebbles on a pond, or riding a roller coaster together.

3. Next Sunday evening, Dad, let your wife know that you would like to take complete responsibility for preparing one of the evening meals during the week. Select the day when it can best fit into your work schedule, or let her choose the night. It will raise the "appreciation quotient" for both of you.

4. Give your spouse a verbal bouquet of compliments. Start by making a list of thirty qualities you appreciate about him or her, and verbally present one each day next month. This may be more difficult than you think. If you run out after five or ten, here are five categories to stimulate your thinking: (1) Character qualities. What about your spouse's personality is most attractive to you? What moral strengths and virtues in your partner do you most admire? What important lessons about life have you learned from him or her? (2) Physical features. (3) Success and achievements. (4) Actions. What does your spouse do for you and the children—including the small things—that

means the most? (5) Talents and skills. Finally, think of as many ways as possible to introduce the compliments: "I love you because . . . ." "I appreciate the way you . . . ." "I'm grateful for . . . ." "I enjoy your . . . ." "You make me feel wonderful when . . . ." "I could never forget your . . . ." "Only you can . . . ." "Have I ever told you that . . . ." "What would I do without your . . . ." "You make me proud when . . . ." And be sure to pay some of the compliments in front of the children, some in front of friends, and the most intimate ones when you are alone together.

5. Have you hugged your husband or wife today? Do it frequently and in front of the children.

6. Single parents especially need to give their children good memories of their childhood. Here are some ideas:

• Notice what your children most enjoy doing and join them in it.

• Decide together what project or sport would make a good family activity, and try it.

• Make your home a place where your children's friends are welcome and come to have fun. When it's appropriate, join in yourself.

• Encourage your children to be open about their thoughts, feelings, and dreams, being sure to create a "safe" environment for them to share themselves with you.

• Frequently retell little anecdotes from when the children were little.

• Take time to enjoy life. You will be sure to give yourself, as well as the kids, many good memories along the way—a heritage especially important to children in a single-parent family.

7 ♂

How to Develop Your Child's Self-Image

ONE OF THE PRIMARY REASONS adolescents get involved in premarital sex is that they have an unhealthy self-image, which can prompt sexual activity. Some teens use sex as a way to increase their self-esteem.

"I used premarital sex to deal with my lack of self-esteem. Each time it proved to me that I was a man and equipped me with good stories for the locker room. I looked to premarital sex to bolster my self-image."

"I looked to female attention for proof of my worth as a male. The attention I received from a young lady became the gauge for my own worth. As I got more physically involved, I found it more difficult to stop at necking and petting and my life became increasingly filled with guilt."

Although both of these statements are from young men, young women with low self-esteem tell similar stories. They become involved sexually to "prove" their worth, to "prove" they can please another person, to "prove" they are attractive to the opposite sex, and to bolster their self-esteem by having experiences to describe to their sexually active peers.

Other young people, however, become sexually active as a way of reinforcing their low view of themselves. They are simply acting out what they believe to be true about themselves. We tend to act in harmony with how we see ourselves. Our self-image is like a set of lenses through which we view all of life. Based on what we see through those lenses, we make choices about what to think and how to act.

If a teenage girl, for example, has low self-esteem and is feeling pressured to become sexually involved, it is easy for her to think, when she looks through her distorted lenses, *I'm not worth much anyway, so what difference does it make? This is what bad people do.* Soon, such a young person is acting out her low opinion of herself.

While building your child's self-image doesn't directly address the issue of sexuality, it is nonetheless one of the most vital ways for you to help prepare your child to say no to sexual pressures.

Getting the Right Perspective

A healthy self-esteem is seeing yourself as God sees you, no more and no less. In other words, a healthy self-image is a realistic view of yourself from God's perspective.

I add the phrase, "no more and no less," to the definition because some people do have an inflated view of themselves, and that's pride. But others have a self-deprecating view of themselves, and that's *false* humility.

In Romans 12:3, Paul says, "I say to every man among you not to think more highly of himself than he ought to think, but to think so as to have sound judgment" (NASB). We ought to think according to sound judgment. That is the truest thing about us.

True humility, which all people with a healthy self-image have, isn't saying, "I'm nothing." Rather, true humility is knowing who you are from God's perspective, accepting yourself as you are, and giving God the glory for it. A healthy self-image includes neither pride nor false humility.

That definition also makes us examine the biblical perspective. If the goal is to see ourselves realistically from God's perspective, we need to know what His perspective is.

First, the Bible tells us that God made man and woman the high point of His creation. Of everything He made, only we were made in His own image (see Gen. 1:27). By itself, this fact of being made in God's image gives each of us great worth. We are very special to Him, much more so than any other part of this universe that He made.

Second, the biblical picture of how much God values us doesn't end with our being made in His image. You are of great value and worth to God. And the simplest and most logical way to tell how much something is worth is to find out how much someone is willing to pay for it. And the great God of the universe considers you and your children to be of such value, even though you are sinners, that He was willing to pay the price of His Son's life to redeem you from the penalty of your sin. Would God have paid that price for a nobody, a worm? No. But He gladly paid it for me, for you, and for our children.

Third, each of us is unique. God created only you to be you, and no one can be *you* better. Each of us and each of our children is unique and priceless. As a parent, you should get in touch with the uniqueness of each of your children and accept each child just as he is. Understanding and appreciating a person's uniqueness will let him or her know that he or she is somebody special.

Finally, the biblical perspective on how we should view ourselves says that we are loved and accepted by God. God tells us, "I have loved you with an everlasting love" (Jer. 31:3) and He accepts us just the way we are. The moment a person puts his or her trust in Jesus Christ as Savior and Lord, the Holy Spirit baptizes that person into the body of Christ. We are accepted in God's family. We belong.

Building a healthy self-image within your child involves three principal elements. It can be likened to a three-legged chair. If you take away or shorten any one of the legs, the chair won't stand upright. Let's look at each of these three "legs" and what you as a parent can do to make your child's "chair" strong.

They Belong

The first leg to developing a healthy self-image within is a sense of belonging or *a feeling of being loved*. We looked at this at some length in chapter 5, but our emphasis there was on how your child needs to sense your acceptance. A child also needs to understand that your acceptance means that they belong. It's the knowledge that someone "really cares for me." Belonging is what I feel when I know I am loved unconditionally, just as I am.

They Are Worthy

The second leg on the chair of healthy self-image is to *feel worthiness*. Whereas belonging means believing others love you unconditionally, worthiness means feeling whole and good about yourself on the inside—a sense that you deserve the love and acceptance of others.

There's a clear connection between belonging and a sense of worthiness. Some children can verbalize these feelings at a surprisingly early age. Others, however, never do understand why they feel unworthy to receive love, and yet they spend a lifetime trying to earn it.

Besides being available to your child, as we mentioned in chapter 5, how do you instill a sense of worthiness? One of the most important things is to be careful how you discipline. When you must discipline your child, be sure to distinguish between the behavior, which may be offensive, and the child himself, your love for whom you must reinforce.

Psychologist Stanley Coopersmith tells in his book *The Antecedent of Self-Esteem* that in his study of children, those with a good sense of self-worth were disciplined as often as those who lacked self-esteem. However, those with a healthy self-esteem were disciplined by their parents for displaying unacceptable *behavior*, whereas those who lacked a healthy self-image were disciplined for being "bad children."

We all have to discipline our children. But when we do, we

should take great care to make this distinction between behavior and personhood. If I were to catch my son Sean lying, for example, the worst thing I could do would be to say something like this: "Sean, you are a liar, and we don't tolerate liars around here. Liars are bad, and we punish them. God said liars will never get to heaven, either." Do you see what that approach will do to a child's sense of being worthy to receive love?

Instead, I should say something like this: "Sean, you are my son and I love you, but you lied to me. Now, your mother and I are not pleased with lying because it dishonors God, it is wrong, and it will ruin your reputation. So, because we love you, you're going to have to be disciplined." This time I focused on his behavior, and at the same time I reaffirmed my love for him and the fact that my discipline grows out of love, not hatred or anger. It's a crucial difference. I've said nothing to suggest he is unworthy of love. In fact, in the midst of the discipline I've reinforced my love for him.

They Are Competent

The third leg on the chair of healthy self-image is having *a feeling of competence*. As children grow and go through life, they need the confidence that they can meet new tasks and challenges successfully. They need the optimism that sees each new day as a fresh set of opportunities to be explored.

Children lacking this sense of competence fear what a new day will bring and what the world will do to them next. Rather than seeing themselves as active in shaping their world and their destiny, they feel inadequate to cope with the world and the problems they face.

I'd like to suggest three ways you can help your child develop a sense of competence. *First,* help your child find at least one area of special competence. If children can feel especially good about their ability in a particular area, it will largely compensate for their inability in other areas. A child who is poor in geometry, for example, may shine in French. A child who lacks athletic gifts may turn out to be an excellent actor. A child who can't play the trumpet may have a strong aptitude for business.

The key here is to help your child find at least one area of competence, then encourage and foster the development of that area. Suppose a girl struggles with school, with music lessons, and with every sport she's ever tried. This is a girl who will have a hard time feeling competent. But then one day she picks up a tennis racket and hits a few balls with some friends. She enjoys it, and lo and behold, she discovers she has a natural aptitude for the game.

The wise parent will see this discovery as a tremendous opportunity to help the girl develop a sense of competence and, with it, a healthy self-image. The parent will praise the girl's accomplishments, buy her a good racket and shoes, find some way to get her good instruction, and make sure she has access to courts for practice time and a way to get there.

Second, you can help your child develop a sense of competence by helping him or her aspire to great things and pursue big dreams, especially when these involve helping others. I'm convinced that those who most enjoy life and have the healthiest self-image are those who have a dream of what they want to be and do and have dedicated their lives to the pursuit of that dream.

If you have a daughter, for example, who wants to be a lawyer in order to help people, help her learn about the various types of work lawyers do, the skills that are most important to a good lawyer, and the kinds of study that would best prepare her for law school. Encourage her to visualize herself doing well and gently guide her in working to make the dream a reality.

It's much easier for children to pursue worthwhile goals if their parents are cheering them on and assuring them they can do it. Persistence can overcome many obstacles, including lack of natural talent. It is young people with a strong sense of competence who will stay with a dream and make it happen. And they need their parents to reinforce the fact that they can be competent.

Helping your child find areas of competence will not only

develop a confidence in his or her competence, but will give him or her a sense of control. A person who feels securely in control of one area—the area of his or her competence—can begin to generalize that sense of control to other areas as well. *If I can do this well in this one area,* a child understands intuitively, *maybe I can exercise some control over other areas of my life, too.*

Third, each person is a special and unique creation of God, the object of His personal attention and indescribable love. The Lord has declared your child to be of incredible worth, so much so that He gave the life of His Son to redeem your child's soul. If you can convey that reality to your child and build on that foundation the three legs of the chair of self-image, then you will have done much to equip your child to make the choice to live a morally pure life.

TRY IT YOURSELF
Ideas for Developing Your Child's Self-Image

Developing a healthy self-image in yourself or others is sort of like building humility—you can't do it by working on the issue itself. You can't say, "I am going to be more humble." Nor can you say, "I'm going to have a healthier self-image." But you can work on some things—doing your best, doing what is right, doing good, sharing your faith, and being thankful, for instance—that will help develop a healthy self-image. Here are some ideas:

1. Words are important, but actions are needed to show your teenager you love him or her. Here are nine ways to show your love for your teenager:

• Do things together, such as biking, backpacking, tennis, Frisbee-throwing in the park, or anything else your child likes to do.

• Attend important events like school athletic games, plays, and open houses.

• With enthusiasm, teach your child to drive.

• Help him or her find an enjoyable job.

• Provide transportation to his or her "dates" with joy and without complaint, especially when it's inconvenient.

• Listen to his or her favorite music and receptively talk about it.

• Make an honest effort to follow his or her friends and their lives.

• Give liberally of your time, presence, and emotional energy.

• Remain approachable by regularly admitting to your own faults and failures.

2. With your spouse, determine one area in which each of your children is particularly competent. Plan how you can encourage that competence in the next week—and do it.

3. Make your own personal influence on your child as strong as possible. Set a good example in your own behavior. If you spend time with your child to maintain a friendship he or she values, your opinion will carry more weight. When you express your own convictions, explain why you have them.

4. Help your child nurture a close relationship with at least one friend who shares his or her values. Teens especially are much more likely to resist "the crowd" when at least one other person stands with them. If your child has such a friend, arrange opportunities for them to spend time together, and especially with your family.

5. Get to know your teen's circle of friends. Invite them to your home often—your influence as a respected adult could extend to them as well.

6. Create challenging situations in which your child will succeed. This can be anything from a tennis game, to a certain goal for report card grades, to helping another person. It can be a group project—participating in a school play, for instance. When your child succeeds, praise him or her profusely, not to convey that your love is conditional on his or her success, but to get him or her in the "success habit."

8 ♂

How to Create an Atmosphere of Forgiveness

A 1983 STUDY AMONG *churched* families by Search Institute found that adolescents in these families prefer to take their problems to their parents rather than to their peers *except* under one condition: when the problem was accompanied with feelings of guilt.

Why do you suppose the adolescents made that exception? Perhaps they don't want to hurt their parents' feelings if they have done something about which they feel guilty. Perhaps they don't want their parents to be disappointed in them. Or perhaps—and I suspect this is a large part of it—they have reason to believe their parents will get upset and make them feel even more guilty, and they understandably want to avoid such a confrontation.

Saying yes to pressures to engage in premarital sex can certainly produce a lot of guilt for young people. In light of that study, then, it's not surprising that our adolescents are hesitant to come to us with their sexual questions and problems. But if they don't come to us with their questions and problems, how are we going to be able to help them?

Building an atmosphere of forgiveness and unconditional acceptance is tough, but crucial. It's relatively easy when the child is loving, cooperative, obedient, and helpful. It's relatively easy because the atmosphere of forgiveness has to be applied only to little things. But for unconditional love and acceptance to be real, it must work for the big things too—when the child is unloving, uncooperative, disobedient, and rebellious. We have discussed several times how we are to convince our child that we love him or her unconditionally. But we can't just talk about it. We must show it.

When our children are small, it's easy to feel love and demonstrate it when they are playful, loving, sweet, and obedient. But do you remember when your child cried most of the night—either because of illness or anger—or threw food when important company was in your home, or wrote on the new wallpaper with a crayon? That was when it was tough to feel love and when it was still more difficult to demonstrate love.

Your kids and mine, just like you and I, are sinners. They *will* make wrong choices. They *will* sometimes be rebellious and defiant. They *will* choose deliberately to sin. It's part of human nature, and it's inevitable. So then the question becomes, how will we as parents react when it happens?

Remember that when a child is rebellious, the principles don't change. Everything we've talked about is still true. It's still true that rules without relationship equal rebellion. It's still true that our children need acceptance, appreciation, availability, affection, and accountability. What's difficult—really tough—is that when our kids make a serious and determined wrong choice, when they are rebellious and defiant over and over again, that's the point more than ever when our children need unconditional love and acceptance. The more erroneous the choice, the more rebellious and defiant the child, the more he or she needs that unconditional love. And yet this is just the time when it's most difficult to give it. That's just the time when it seems like offering unconditional love is a waste of time. But believe me it's not.

Please understand, I'm not condoning sin or saying parents shouldn't discipline. We need to set appropriate rules to guide the conduct of our children, and we should discipline in love when the rules are broken. But unless we maintain a spirit of forgiveness we can add to their burden of guilt and drive them away emotionally and spiritually. Yet as they see our brokenness and feel our forgiving heart it can invite repentance and bring healing between them and us and between them and the Lord.

To maintain a relationship with our adolescents and be in a position to help them say no to sexual pressures, we need to build an atmosphere of forgiveness, not condemnation. It's the only way they will come to us when the pressure is on, and especially when they have already made a mistake.

If the atmosphere you have created in your home to this point has not been one of forgiveness, you won't be able to change it overnight. And it may need to begin with your asking your child to forgive *you* for things you have said and done in the past. But if you will begin today to work at following up your unconditional acceptance with forgiveness, you can over time create an atmosphere in which your child will come to you with even the most difficult problems, an atmosphere in which you consistently offer godly pardon.

Our Prodigal Children

I mentioned earlier that our children will make wrong decisions. As free moral agents with wills of their own, they will sin. You can love all you want and establish healthy boundaries, but they will still make their own decisions at the point of temptation. Accordingly, I am firmly convinced that we can be the finest parents in the world, do everything by the book, and our children can still choose to indulge in premarital sex.

When our children are rejecting Christian teaching and our rules in that way, what do we do? Lock them in their rooms and throw away the key? Preach at them from sunup to sunset? Send them to a military school and hope the school can better control them? I believe we have a good model for how to respond in Jesus' parable of the prodigal son, found in Luke 15.

The prodigal son represents each of us at some point in

our lives or maybe at times every day, while the father represents God. Given that, it's safe to assume that the young man was reared in a warm, loving family where he knew unconditional acceptance, forgiveness, and parental appreciation and availability—all the things that make for good relationships and a healthy self-image.

In spite of that, however, this young free moral agent decided to collect his share of the family inheritance, get away from the rules and religious values of his parents, and go have a "good time."

That was his plan. His loving father knew what he was likely to do with his money, but what was his response? More rules? Preaching? Grounding until the boy came to his senses? "So he divided to them [his two sons] his livelihood" (v. 12). This was not what we might have expected. Would you have done the same? I'm not sure I would have.

This father knew, however, that all the preaching in the world wasn't going to dissuade a young person from doing what he had really made up his mind to do. He might at first have tried to talk the boy out of it, but it was soon obvious the young man wouldn't listen.

You know what happened next. The son wasted all his money on "prodigal living" (v. 13), and I'll let you use your own imagination as to what that included. Different translations of the Bible use the words "loose living," "riotous living," and "wild living." Eventually he ran out of money, and at the same time the country where he was living was hit by a famine. In a classic understatement, the Bible says he "began to be in want" (v. 14).

As a result, the young man was forced to take the only job he could get—feeding swine—which would have been an utter disgrace to a young Jew like him. And as he sat there in the field, he "came to himself" (v. 17) and decided to return to his father, admit his sin, beg forgiveness, and ask for a job as a hired hand.

This young man knew his father had always loved and accepted and forgiven him in the past. When he had wanted to leave home, his father by his actions had communicated unconditional acceptance and forgiveness. That's the crucial point to bear in mind. He decided to return home after he had experienced the futility of his lifestyle *because he had good reason to believe his father would forgive him* and at least let him live as a servant.

If my child went off and did what this young man did, living immorally and wasting half of what I had worked my whole life to build, would he have good reason to believe, if he came to his senses, that he would find a welcome of forgiveness when he got home? Or would I say, "I told you so!"?

And so the young man headed for home. When he arrived, his father wasn't just taking care of business. No, Jesus said that while "he [the son] was still a great way off, his father saw him" (v. 20). How did the father see him from a distance? I can imagine he was on top of the highest hill around, stretching up on tiptoes to try to catch the first glimpse of the return of his beloved son. And he was probably up there every day, looking and hoping.

Note that the Bible says nothing about the father's trying to track down his son while the young man was living in sin. He didn't try to prevent him from wasting his life, and he also didn't bail him out when he got in trouble. Rather, he waited for his son to reach the place where he decided for himself to repent and head for home.

"His father saw him and had compassion, and ran and fell on his neck and kissed him" (v. 20). The son then tried to give his prepared speech of repentance, but the father interrupted and said to his servants, "Bring out the best robe and put it on him, and put a ring on his hand [symbolic of the family's authority] and sandals on his feet. And bring the fatted calf here and kill it, and let us eat and be merry, for this my son was dead and is alive again; he was lost and is found" (vv. 22–24).

There you have God's blueprint for handling a rebellious child. It's not easy to follow, I know. When that child walks out the door intent on sinning, he puts your reputation and standing in the church and community on the line along with his own. But even more than that, you know better than he how badly he may be hurt and may hurt others in the process.

These are all concerns that will stay with us. We can't stop them forever from doing what they are intent upon. Nor can we always save them, even if we should try to, from the consequences of their bad decisions. What we can do is implant in them before they go the assurance that home is a place of forgiveness as well as acceptance. And then if they should make their way home again, we can welcome them with open arms of love.

Rules and Relationship

Suppose a child is rebelling but not leaving home. What should be our approach? Let me mention again the central theme of this book: rules without relationship equal rebellion. Although it certainly won't be easy—it will go against our natural inclination—what we must do is ease back on the rules and build the relationship. We need to work at offering acceptance, appreciation, availability, affection, and accountability.

In other words, we need to convince our children that we are on their side. By action as well as words, we need to show them that our love and acceptance really are unconditional, and that our forgiveness is always available if they will but ask. We need to remind our children gently that the same is true of God. And then we have to step back and, if necessary, let them learn their lessons the hard way, including how to live with the consequences of their decisions.

In the meantime, every day in our hearts we climb to the top of the hill and look for even the faintest sign that our child has come to his or her senses and is on the way home.

Teaching Forgiveness Early

From a child's earliest interaction with Mom and Dad after an act of disobedience, the child begins to learn whether his love and acceptance are conditional or unconditional; whether a distinction is made between behavior, which may be bad, and the child himself. They soon will determine whether Mom and Dad can be trusted to provide forgiveness as a way out of guilt. Thus, ideally, a child is learning how to find forgiveness from his first days.

However, if your child is older, perhaps already an adolescent, and you haven't created an atmosphere of forgiveness before, please don't despair. Just begin now to build that kind of environment for your child. It won't be easy and it won't happen instantly. There will be setbacks along the way. But God can clear away the mistakes of the past and give you and your child a fresh start out of His own forgiveness. In fact, God specializes in doing just that.

TRY IT YOURSELF
Ideas for Creating an Atmosphere of Forgiveness

1. Is there anything God could not or would not forgive? Is there anything you could do that God would not forgive you if you repented? Is there anything you could do that Mom and Dad would not forgive you for? Discuss these and other questions about forgiveness with your children, perhaps at dinner. Through these discussions, you will have an opportunity to build an understanding of forgiveness in your children.

2. One of the hardest tasks a parent has is to create an atmosphere of forgiveness, to let the child know that even though he or she has "blown it," Mom and Dad still love and accept him or her unconditionally. It helps for them to know we are in constant need of forgiveness. Share openly some times when you've "blown it" and needed the unconditional love and acceptance of someone too.

King David is a good example of someone who "blew it." He was the king of Israel, God's hand was on him, he had everything going for him. And then he saw Bathsheba and was hooked. The Bible says "and he lay with her . . . and the woman conceived." Since her husband Uriah was off in battle,

David decided he had to get Uriah home so that Uriah would think the child was his own. Unfortunately for David, Uriah was so committed to the king that he would not go to bed with his wife while he was supposed to be in battle. And so David devised a plan in which Uriah was killed.

When the prophet Nathan confronted David, David confessed his sins:

> Have mercy upon me, O God,
> According to Your lovingkindness;
> According to the multitude of Your tender mercies,
> Blot out my transgressions.
> Wash me thoroughly from my iniquity.
> And cleanse me from my sin.
>
> For I acknowledge my transgressions,
> And my sin is ever before me.
> Against You, You only, have I sinned,
> And done this evil in Your sight—
> That You may be found just when You speak,
> And blameless when You judge.
>
> Behold, I was brought forth in iniquity,
> And in sin my mother conceived me.
> Behold, You desire truth in the inward parts,
> And in the hidden part You will make me to know wisdom.
>
> Purge me with hyssop, and I shall be clean;
> Wash me, and I shall be whiter than snow.
> Make me to hear joy and gladness,
> That the bones which You have broken may rejoice.
> Hide Your face from my sins,
> And blot out all my iniquities.
>
> Create in me a clean heart, O God,
> And renew a steadfast spirit within me.
> Do not cast me away from Your presence,
> And do not take Your Holy Spirit from me.
>
> Restore to me the joy of Your salvation,
> And uphold me with Your generous Spirit.

Then I will teach transgressors Your ways,
And sinners shall be converted to You. (Ps. 51:1–13)

Here are several steps for you to take when you sin. Practice them because when your child "blows it" and comes to you, you can tell him or her how to restore their relationship with God:

a. *Acknowledge the sin.* So many people say, "God, I've sinned . . . but I loved her . . . but I was vulnerable." Rather say, "God, I have sinned." Admit your sin before God.

b. *Show fruits of repentance.* Repentance means turning around, changing one's mind. Matthew 3:8 says, "bear fruits worthy of repentance." It might mean breaking off a relationship or perhaps making a decision not to be alone together. It might be something else. Whatever it is, there should be fruits in line with repentance.

c. *Acknowledge Christ's forgiveness.* First John 1:9 says, "If we confess our sins, He is faithful and just to forgive us our sins and to cleanse us from all unrighteousness." Hebrews 10:12 mentions that Christ's death is "one sacrifice for sins forever." Christ's forgiveness can make you whole again. First acknowledge the sin; then show fruits of repentance; then acknowledge Christ's forgiveness.

d. *Forgive yourself.* Often when I sin, I know God can forgive me, but I say, "Oh, McDowell, you shouldn't have done or said that" and I don't forgive myself. If you are not willing to forgive yourself, you are saying two things to God: (1) Christ's death was not sufficient, and (2) you are a higher judge of what can be forgiven than God is. God's grace is extended to us out of His heart of love and when we do not forgive ourselves, we throw God's grace right back into His face. If God's grace can't cover the sin in our lives, it can't cover any sin.

e. *Don't let Satan deceive you.* Satan, the great deceiver, will try to make you feel condemned. But if you are trusting Jesus Christ as your Savior, you cannot be condemned. The Bible says, "There is therefore now no condemnation to those who are in Christ Jesus" (Rom. 8:1). But be sure to discern the difference between condemnation and conviction. When sin enters into your life, the Holy Spirit doesn't work to condemn you, but He does work to convict you. Satan's condemnation pulls you away from Christ and leads you to despair. The Holy Spirit's conviction draws you to Christ and leads you to joy.

Practice these steps to restoring your relationship to God when you sin. You need to do it for your own sake and you need to be able to speak from experience when your son or daughter needs guidance.

Further resources: His Image—My Image and *The Secret of Loving.*

9 ♂

How to Instill Christian Values

"I GREW UP IN A NEIGHBORHOOD which consisted of about twelve guys, all one to three years older than I," said a young man I'll call Ron. "Every weekend we'd get together to play sports, work on our cars, talk about girls. Every weekend my mind was bombarded with the same general presuppositions about manhood: real men must be having sex with anyone and everyone.

"As I continued to listen to the older guys brag about their conquests, I began to fantasize about what it would be like for me."

Lacking objective values that said premarital sex is always wrong and not realizing the truth that everyone *isn't* having sex, Ron soon became sexually active himself. And a few years later, he found himself waiting in his car outside the community hospital while his girlfriend was inside being tested for pregnancy. It had been two and a half months since her last period, and they both feared the worst.

"I was terrified," Ron said. "My mind was going crazy with all kinds of things. What if someone she knows sees her getting a pregnancy checkup? Gossip will spread like wildfire. What if she *is* pregnant? I don't believe in abortion, but getting rid of the evidence is sure better than suffering the embarrassment of having to get married!"

"Married? Do I really love this girl enough to get married? She's the best thing that's ever happened to me, but I'm not ready to spend the rest of my life with her."

"What about my parents? They worked so hard to develop a good reputation in the community. They'll be crushed. Then there are my neighbors and the people at church. All this time they thought I was such a fine, upstanding young man."

Fortunately, the girlfriend wasn't pregnant, but she and Ron continued to have sex for another year until he became a Christian. Apparently, though, he was going to church all the time he was sexually active before his conversion. And what does Ron think of his premarital sexual activity now?

"As I reflect on this terrifying experience, I have come to realize my whole life could have been ruined, all because *I chose to respond to some false thinking I picked up from other guys way back in junior high.*"

Ron grew up, he said, "with the general presuppositions about manhood [that] real men must be having sex with anyone and everyone." We've seen that the media bombard you, me, and our children with the same message. And if our children have the same presuppositions about manhood that Ron had, they will either act in such a way as to be a "real man" or "real woman" or they will have a low self-esteem because they aren't fulfilling their ideal of a "real man" or a "real woman." They may also be living a life of frustration because they can't (or feel they shouldn't) do what a "real man" or a "real woman" would do.

A Christian's View of Sex

The solution rests with our children internalizing a Christian perspective instead of accepting the world's presuppositions. Instilling this Christian perspective in our children is one of the most important legacies we can leave them and a significant factor in helping them to say no to premarital sex.

Let's consider four specific ways, all having to do with relationships, in which the Christian perspective, or agenda, ought to be different from the world's agenda. Looking at them in this way will identify some of the values we want to instill in our children.

First, the Christian believes that each person is special and of great worth because each one is made in the image of God. This means that every individual deserves dignity, respect, and consideration. In practical terms, a boy who lives with a Christian agenda will give dignity, respect, and consideration to his girlfriend.

Second, because each person has great worth, the Christian believes we should not manipulate people to please ourselves or to get our needs met at their expense. To use people cheapens them. It implies that we think we are better than they are, that they don't deserve any better treatment from us.

We should teach our children this value so that when they are tempted to use someone, or when someone else tries to manipulate them, alarm bells will go off and they will realize what's happening. For example, when a girl hears her boyfriend say, "If you really loved me, you would make love to me," she should recognize that he is trying to use her. She will know that not only does he not love her, but he doesn't think much of her either.

The *third* value a Christian believes and which we should instill in our children is that we should treat others with the love and respect God gives to us, the same appreciation we would like to receive from others. What's this love like?

"Love suffers long and is kind; love does not envy; love does not parade itself, is not puffed up; does not behave rudely, does not seek its own, is not provoked, thinks no evil; does not rejoice in iniquity, but rejoices in the truth; bears all things, believes all things, hopes all things, endures all things. Love never fails" (1 Cor. 13:4–8).

This scripture pretty well describes the way God loves us and that is the kind of love you would like to receive from others. You should therefore give others the same quality of love. "Whatever you want men to do to you, do also to them" (Matt. 7:12).

Fourth, a Christian believes in the value of waiting. "Love is patient" (1 Cor. 13:4). In God's perfect plan for us, there is a proper time and place for everything, including, as Ecclesiastes 3:5 says, "A time to embrace, And a time to refrain from embracing."

Today, not much value is placed on patience, on waiting for anything. If you want to do or own something, don't wait, we're told. Go out and do it now or buy it now. You don't have the cash to pay for it? No problem. Just pull out your charge card and sign on the dotted line. Advertising fuels this message, and merchants live off it.

The same is true of relationships. Our world asks, are you lonely? Do you feel a need for intimacy? Are you curious about sex? No problem. There is no need to wait for marriage.

There is a time and a place for sexual intimacy and pleasure, a time and place that God honors and which is best for us. That time and place is the marriage bed.

Teach Naturally and Casually

It is important to know the values or presuppositions we want to instill in our children, but we also need to consider the two ways in which we can actually instill these values in them. The first is the most important way we instill anything in our kids—by example. The behavior, speech, and attitudes we *model* are the ones we will see most often in them.

Therefore, I begin by examining myself as I examine myself daily, to see what attitudes, speech, and behavior I am displaying before my child. Actions speak louder than words—so much so that the words are in most cases a waste of breath if they're inconsistent with our actions.

But it is not enough to model Christian values. There is a need for deliberate, systematic teaching of them as well. Making the time to explain the values by which we live and why we think they will serve our children's best interests is time well spent.

Teaching takes place most easily in casual, relaxed settings. For example, mealtimes offer excellent opportunities to teach. When I'm home, I always take my children out for breakfast on the way to school. To keep the cost down, we'll order one item and share it. I'll read a biblical passage, explain briefly what it teaches, and then ask my kids hypothetical questions that apply the principles.

Dinner time at home can offer an equally good opportunity for discussion. But whenever we want to teach, we have to plan ahead. Good teaching and discussion don't happen automatically. If you were at work and were given the most important assignment of your career, you would certainly prepare diligently and then give it the very best effort of which you are capable. The fact is that there is no more important assignment we will ever have than to instill Christian values in our children.

Long walks, travel time in the car, and just the everyday occurrences of life also offer excellent opportunities to instill values. Suppose, for example, that you buy something in a store and the clerk gives you too much change. Don't just return the overpayment, but use the opportunity to say to your child who's shopping with you, "I returned that money that didn't rightfully belong to me for a couple of reasons, Honey. First, because it's the honest thing to do, and God would want me to do that because He always tells the truth, doesn't He?

"I also returned the money because the clerk could get in trouble at the end of the day if he doesn't have as much cash in his drawer as he's supposed to. So the kind thing to do is to return it. Besides, if I were in his place, I'd sure want the money returned."

A good book to refer to in teaching values to your children is *Forty Ways to Teach Your Child Values* by Paul Lewis (Tyndale House Publishers). As we instill values through this kind of informal teaching, we want our children to begin using Christian values to evaluate everything they see and hear. These values should become a sort of filter through which our children see the world. To help get your child into that habit, do some things together and then discuss them in light of the Christian perspective. Watch television together, read the same books, go to an occasional movie—or listen to popular songs—together. Ask, "What perspective is this show (or movie, or book, or song) advocating? How does it compare to our Christian values?"

Younger children will love spending this kind of time with you, but adolescents may be more difficult. They will appreciate the attention, especially if you are consistent in giving it, but it may seem awkward when you first try to do it. Stay with it. You and your child will both get used to it and end up having some great times together.

TRY IT YOURSELF
Ideas for Resetting Your Child's Agenda

Resetting your child's agenda depends on how old he or she is and how much the child has already been molded by the world.

For younger children

1. Be aware of opportunities to teach your children the Christian values we discussed. Have as your goal to be aware enough to create at least one teaching situation tomorrow. At first this will seem forced, but as it becomes a habit with you—without being preachy—it will become more natural.

2. Write your own book one evening this week. Pick a theme like "Success is . . . ," "Love is . . . ," "Dreams are . . . ," "Faith is . . . " or other themes like taking a risk, being a friend, or fathers and mothers. (What topic would you like to know your child's beliefs about?) Make a simple statement, draw or paste a picture under it on each page, and ask your child to add to the statement.

3. To teach honesty, ask what your child would do if he saw one of his or her friends slip a small pencil sharpener into his lunch sack while in a stationery store. Follow with questions like "Why?" and "What would result?"

For older children

1. The Christian's agenda and the world's agenda ought to be different. Discuss that fact with your children, not to identify details, but to establish it as a fact. Then, with the premise established, let your children identify various practical ways in which the Christian's agenda and the world's agenda are different. Covenant with your children that you and they will demonstrate a Christian agenda—in the ways you and they have defined it—instead of a worldly one.

2. One night this week explore family values by asking each person to go to his room for five minutes to think about this question: If a flood, tornado, or fire were going to destroy your home and all of your possessions, which ones would you grab to take out with you? When you reassemble, tell what you picked and why. Cap the time by discussing the things you realize the family could do without. Discuss what this statement means: "There are people who know the cost of everything and the value of nothing."

3. To encourage thinking about honesty, discuss a newspaper article which reports various acts of dishonesty. Help your teens discern the motivations for such acts. Guide them to see that without honesty, we can't get along in the relationships of life—school, home, marriage, community, and government.

4. If you need to create a good situation where you and your teenager can talk, invite him or her to a meal. There are very few adolescent males, for instance, who would resist a free meal.

10 ♂

How to Reinforce Positive Influences

HAVE YOU EVER THOUGHT about how little time you and your spouse actually get to spend with your school-age child in a typical week? Much of each day from Monday through Friday, your child is in school. More time is used as your child walks, drives, rides a bike, or takes a bus to and from school.

Before school, of course, everyone in the family is running around trying to get ready for the day. After school, your child may be involved in extracurricular activities, a job, or social activities. If you are a single parent, or both you and your spouse work outside the home, you may not see your child before dinner even if he or she does come straight home after classes. On weekends, if your child is an adolescent, he or she is probably busy much of the time with friends, work, or dating.

When we stop to tally the time, we probably have only a few minutes or hours at best during the week when we can have much direct input into our children's lives. Who are the other people who spend time with our children and undoubtedly exert a significant influence on them?

In years past, a child was influenced not only by his or her parents, but by grandparents, aunts, and uncles who were living in the same house or nearby. But the mobility and urbanization of our society have made the extended family living in proximity to each other largely a thing of the past. I don't mean to romanticize our past, but it is true that children had more influence from other family members when we were a more rural and less mobile society. Today as parents we are pretty much on our own and need to see to it that when our children aren't under our influence, the influence they *are* under will help support rather than undermine our values.

Positive Peer Pressure

Peer pressure is usually thought of as a negative influence, and it often is. But if we help our children find good peer groups, it can actually be a very positive thing. For example, my son, Sean, has been part of several soccer teams over the past few years that have provided peer pressure as good as I could hope for. The kids on these teams have been a great influence on him. It has helped that some of the coaches have been Christian men, but this is not essential for good peer influence. We should seek out this kind of experience for our children whenever it is possible.

Other places where your child might find positive peer pressure are in Boy Scouts or Girl Scouts, the YWCA or YMCA, Boys Clubs, 4-H, a church youth group, or some after-school activities such as sports, drama, band, ballet, or the school newspaper.

Don't assume, however, that just because our children are involved in a good activity, they are necessarily under good influence. Take the time to get to know his coaches, advisers, and group leaders, as well as the other kids in the group. You might even invite them over to dinner to become better acquainted with them. I'm not saying you should give them the third degree or immediately withdraw your child from the group if the others involved aren't Christians. But you should know what input your child is receiving and how to counter any negative influence if necessary.

It is also important, of course, that we be continually talking to our children about their activities and friends. If we have built the kind of relationship we talked about in chapter 5, we should have the quality of communication that lets us know pretty well how things are going.

School and Teachers

In addition to peers, a child's teachers certainly rank near the top of the list of influential people in his or her life. We will want to take advantage of opportunities like parent-teacher conferences, PTA meetings, and parent auxiliaries at school to know our children's teachers. If there are any problems at any time, don't hesitate to call a teacher and arrange a meeting.

Most teachers are caring professionals who want to do a good job. Needless to say you may certainly come across teachers who don't share your Christian values. Remember that, intentionally or not, all teachers, by example if nothing else, promote their values to their students.

Look carefully, also, at the content of textbooks and courses. We need to know what ideas and values are being formally presented to our children. Although some professional educators want to argue this point, the fact remains that our children's education is primarily *our* concern and *our* responsibility, not the teachers'. As parents we have a right not to have our values undercut by what the school is teaching. So don't be afraid to object if you find offensive material in what your child is being taught.

Latchkey Kids and Single Parenting

The phenomenon of the latchkey kid is growing steadily in this country, and it presents another parenting challenge. If your child is going to be home for several hours without adult supervision, who or what will be exerting influence over her or him during that time? Will it be peers, soap operas on television, rock music on the stereo, or something else?

You should also know that whereas the back seat of a car used to be the most popular place for adolescent sexual activity, that's no longer the case. Today, the most common place is at home, in the afternoon from 3 to 5, when the kids are home from school and Mom and Dad are still at work.

What are your options? You can try to get your child involved in an activity such as a sport, drama, club, or an after-school job. Or perhaps you can find a nearby relative, neighbor, or friend who is home and to whose house your child can go after classes, a place where your child will be supervised by a good adult role model.

If you are a single parent, you can help your child by finding some "para-parents" to get involved with him or her. These people should be a stable and loving married couple who can spend time with your child and exert a good influence. Among other things, they can show your child what a solid and loving marriage relationship looks like. A good place to look for such people is in your church; your pastor might be able to suggest a couple.

Even if your own marriage is solid, if you live at a distance from grandparents, you might want to find some "adoptive" grandparents for your child. These should be people who can spend time with your child, model a strong marriage, and share the wisdom of their years. Such people can also be a tremendous blessing to the single parent.

The Power of Books

While we must seek to provide our children with a healthy circle of contacts, let's also realize that we can influence the development of their thinking through what they read. Try to develop in your child a love of great books, including the Bible. Most young children love to read, and that's a love that should be continually encouraged. Great books can occupy a child, including an adolescent, for hours at a time. And they can serve to teach and reinforce the Christian values you want your child to make his own, too.

I would particularly suggest you introduce your older child to biographies and journals of some of the marvelous saints of the past: Hudson Taylor, Dwight Moody, Jonathan Edwards, Jim Elliot, George Whitefield, Dawson Trotman, Augustine, Billy Sunday, Eric Liddell, John Bunyan, and C. S. Lewis, to name just a few. Reading about these spiritual giants, their mistakes as well as their accomplishments, can be a tremendous example and inspiration to your child. Also, biographies of Christian sports figures and music artists can be extremely helpful.

No, being a parent today isn't easy, not in our post-Christian culture, and not when we really have very little time with a school-age child. But with some thought, planning, and effort, we can surround our children with a healthy circle of contacts that will reinforce the Christian values we are carefully teaching.

TRY IT YOURSELF
**Ideas for Encompassing Your Child with a
Healthy Circle of Contacts**

Here are some suggestions that have helped other parents:

1. Select a church with a healthy youth group.

2. It is also possible to select a good Christian school in some areas.

3. Check out various organizations and activities available to children within your area, i.e., Youth for Christ, Student Venture, Young Life, Fellowship of Christian Athletes, etc.

4. Attend church conferences and camps. This has helped our family.

5. Find out where families go whose children you would like to influence your kids, and send your children to the camps they attend.

6. Arrange your own "great escapes" to places where these families go.

7. One concerned mother in our community organized a group of children whose parents she knew and respected. They would meet monthly for special activities that would excite the children, such as roller skating parties, beach parties, trips to museums, etc. The young people in her group even collected used clothing and took it to needy people in Mexico. In all of this, she sought the help of other parents.

8. We also had family outings with other families whose children we wanted to influence ours.

9. One final personal suggestion: as parents my wife and I made a commitment to "bus" friends from outside the neighborhood to our home to play with our children. At times this may be inconvenient, but it's worth the effort if you want to reinforce positive influences in the lives of your children.

11 ☿

How to Teach Sex

I LIVE OUTSIDE SAN DIEGO, up in the mountains. One time, because my wife was busy, my secretary came to the airport to pick me up after a trip and she brought my two oldest children with her. I figured this was a great chance to spend an hour and a half with my children, and so I asked her to do the driving. I got in back with Kelly, who was ten at the time, and Sean, who was eight.

As we drove away from the airport, I started our conversation, as I often do when I return home from a trip, by telling them how lucky I am to be their father and to have their mother as my wife. Before long, as so commonly happens with kids, they got into a little argument. In the middle of their spat, my angelic, eight-year-old Sean said to his sister, "F___ you!"

My secretary immediately and visibly tensed up and began glancing in the rearview mirror, no doubt eager to see how I would respond.

How would most parents respond in that situation? When I ask that question in high school and college assemblies, the kids quickly answer that their parents would say things like "Shut up! That's nasty. Dirty. Filthy. I'm going to wash your mouth out with soap if you ever say that again." Often that's what you would expect, right?

However, I saw Sean's words as a golden opportunity to

teach. Sean obviously didn't know what the word meant. If I had jumped on him and told him how dirty the word was, he would have learned not only that the word was bad, but he would also have had a negative impression about the sex act itself when he learned what it was.

So instead I said, "Son, where did you learn that word?"

"On the school bus," he answered.

"Do you know what it means?" I asked.

"No," he said.

"Can I explain it to you, then?" I said.

"Yeah!" he answered. "What is it?" He was dying to know.

And for the next forty minutes, I had a fabulous opportunity to teach my son and daughter about the sanctity, the beauty, and the purpose of sex. It was an opportunity for which I am extremely grateful, an experience I'll never forget—nor, I suspect, will they.

The next morning, I learned it wasn't only my children whom I taught during that ride in the car. My secretary, a woman in her early twenties at the time, came over to our house and had coffee with Dottie. She explained that she had grown up in a Christian home and an evangelical church. She was ready to get married. But she told Dottie that she had learned more about sex in one hour in the car as I explained it to my children the day before than she had in her entire life from her parents.

This story illustrates several important points. *First,* and most important, is the fact that proper sex education, or what I prefer to call "life education," is vital and ought to come from parents before it comes from anyone else. Teaching our children about sex is part of our overall responsibility and thrilling privilege as parents to prepare them for life and the proper enjoyment of God's gifts.

Second, the first time a parent teaches a child about sex should not be in a formal setting as the child approaches puberty—"the big talk"—but natural opportunities to tell children what they are ready to hear. If you have given your child a good sex education when he or she is growing up, "the big talk" will never be necessary.

Third, unfortunately sex education is ignored by most parents, both Christian and non-Christian, out of discomfort, ignorance, or indifference. According to surveys, most adolescents report they have *never* been given *any* advice about sex by either parent. In another study, "Only about one-third of the adolescents surveyed reported that they had 'good talks with my parents about sex.'"

One young person wrote to me that "parents need to be more active in the process of their child's developing sexual maturity. Lines of communication need to be opened with the child about his understanding of sex and the feelings swirling around inside him or her, as the door to the sexual world is opened. The parent should be there to offer guidance and point the child in the right direction. Letting a child get into a situation that he or she is not emotionally ready to handle can very easily lead to devastation. In a young adolescent, the mind is often not as mature as the body. Parents need to be involved in each stage of the child's changing sexuality."

When to Begin

The sex education of our children needs to begin at a very early age—in one sense, virtually from birth. Through their very early years, we need to let our children know that the body is a wonderful gift from God, and all bodily functions and parts are normal and nothing to be ashamed of. When children touch their private parts in play during bath time, for example, as they will do, they shouldn't have their hands slapped and told that they are doing something dirty. In the proper context, sex is a natural and healthy part of life, and that's the impression we ought to give our children—not that sex is some mysterious and somehow ugly thing.

Actual discussion and verbal teaching about sex needs to begin as early as three or four years of age, and certainly no later than six or seven. As we've already seen, we live in a sex-obsessed and sex-saturated culture, which means our children are being exposed to sexual information *from other sources.* Whether we like it or not, they are getting input from the media and other parts of society as soon as they start watching television or interacting with neighborhood children.

The question, then, isn't whether our children will receive some kind of sex education in their earliest years. They will. *The only thing up in the air is whether they will learn first from us or from our culture.*

As a parent, you should be the one molding your child's perception of sex, not anybody else. Let us not let anyone or anything rob us of the joy of shaping our children's perception of sex in a healthy, biblical, and God-honoring way.

Remember, too, that children want to learn from their parents. The younger they are, the more they want Mom and Dad to teach them about life and everything in it. Take advantage of your child's desire. Bear in mind, too, that it's always more difficult to correct wrong thinking than to prevent it. If we begin to teach our children the proper perspective early, we can save both us and our children a lot of grief later.

Another reason to begin teaching our children without delay is that as children grow older, it becomes increasingly difficult to have frank discussions. As children mature, and especially as they approach puberty, their natural and healthy individuality grows, and they value their privacy more and more. To try to talk about sex at that point can be perceived by a child as a serious invasion of privacy if there is not already a foundation in place for it.

Under no circumstances, however, should we allow a boy or girl to reach puberty with all its difficulties without our having explained carefully what's going to happen and what it means. If a child lacks such an understanding, the onset of menstruation or ejaculation can be a terribly frightening experience. We shouldn't try to guess when our children will reach puberty and then have a "big talk" just before it happens, either. We need to prepare our children well in advance.

What to Say

When it comes to specifically what we should teach our children and at what ages, the operative principle is that little questions deserve little answers; big questions deserve big answers; and frank questions deserve frank answers. Tailor what you teach, in other words, to the age and actual question of the child. Loading down a young child with too much information too soon can cause confusion and anxiety.

A seven-year-old boy once asked his mother, "Where did I come from?" The mother, as often happens in that situation, got embarrassed and stumbled through a rather lengthy explanation of his sexual origin. The little boy found his mother's answer puzzling, and after she finished he said, "Well, Tommy told me *he* came from Philadelphia."

First, in teaching our children, we need to use proper language right from the beginning. Call a penis a penis and a vagina a vagina; don't use any cute little terms. For several reasons this is more necessary than it used to be. For one thing, because of all the sexual information in society, our children will be hearing about these things anyway. Teach the proper terms so that our children will know what these names are.

Second, we want to teach our children respect for sex and the relationship of which it's a part. And respect is conveyed by the use of proper language, not the slang or vulgarity our children are going to pick up if left to themselves to learn about sex. Our choice of language actually colors our thinking. If a boy begins to think and talk about his penis using the crude terms the world employs, for example, he's already forming a picture of sex in his mind as something cheap and vulgar— something far from the beautiful expression of marital love that God intended.

Third, we want to teach our children the proper terms because if we can't, if we are too uncomfortable or embarrassed to say "vagina," for instance, our children will pick up our feelings and also be embarrassed to speak frankly and reverently about sex. Again, we want them to think of sex as normal and natural and healthy as long as it's kept in the right contex of a loving marriage relationship. It's not something of whicl we need ever be ashamed in that setting.

Regarding the biological facts of sex and reproductior that we will need to teach our children, we may feel inadequate because we are lacking knowledge. If that's the case, don't be embarrassed, just go get the facts. They are readily available from many books at the library, a bookstore, or from you family doctor. Remember, we are on an important mission—to fulfill our obligation as parents to educate our children—anc many other people who recognize just how important that is will be glad to help.

In the way of books that will help you prepare to teacl your child, there is one book in particular that I'd recommend. It's titled simply *Almost Twelve*, and the author is Ken Taylor the man who paraphrased *The Living Bible*.

As your child grows older and matures in the ability tc think logically, you should also teach him or her to think aheac about the *consequences* of his or her words and actions, espe cially in the area of sex. Our society urges all of us to seek instant gratification of every desire. If you want to own some thing, buy it now with credit. If you want to do something that feels good, do it now—grab all the gusto you can!

What gets left out of this overwhelming focus on the pleasure of the moment is that words spoken and actions taker today do have consequences tomorrow. Uncontrolled use of credit leads to financial bondage at the least and bankruptcy at the worst. Giving in to the sexual urge outside of marriage car lead to pregnancy, venereal disease, and emotional scars that last a lifetime. Thus, our children need a forward-looking per spective. They need to learn to think not only of the possible pleasure of the moment, but also of the likely consequences of what they say and do. And nowhere is this more important than in the area of sexual involvement.

Next, we need to teach our children that character is judged by what people say and do. And the quality of a person's love life—not just sex, but the whole relationship including marriage—is just a reflection of his or her overall character. Thus, when a person uses foul language with sexual connotations to degrade someone, he's revealing that he has a very low opinion of sex and certainly doesn't respect it the way God intended.

A person's language reveals his opinion of sex. We need to urge our children to think carefully about their own use of language. Their alert ears take in a lot of profanity and vulgarity, and it's easy for young people to fall into the habit of speaking the same way if they don't stop to think about what they're saying and what it says about their character. In addition, the Bible says, "Whatever things are true, whatever things are noble, whatever things are just, whatever things are pure, whatever things are lovely, whatever things are of good report, if there is any virtue and if there is anything praiseworthy— meditate on these things" (Phil. 4:8). Profanity and vulgarity are hardly noble, just, and pure.

Always teach sex education in a context of values, never as mere biology. We should remind our children that sex is a gift of God for the committed bond of marriage. What we do sexually involves our relationship with God. Premarital sex violates His commands. On the positive side, His commands are all for our good. He knows and wants only what's best for us, not a cheap substitute.

How to Say It

I've already said that the typical "big talk" approach to teaching sex education is too little too late. So how do we do it? Very simply, we should take advantage of the many little, natural opportunities that come along. First, of course, our children will ask many questions. Seize these chances; don't see them as crises or embarrassments.

However, we shouldn't be surprised if questions come at embarrassing moments, such as the night the pastor is over for dinner or when you are in the middle of the grocery store. Kids seem to have a sixth sense about the most interesting timing for such questions.

You can also look for natural opportunities to teach when your child doesn't ask a question. On a visit to the zoo, for example, talk about the bear cub and how he got there. When you and your child see an obviously pregnant woman, talk about that. The fact is that teaching about sex by answering questions which come up is far easier on you as the parent.

Another chance I had to teach Kelly and Sean a few years ago demonstrates the way in which you can capitalize on a situation. My family and I were in Venice, California one day and we had the afternoon free. Venice is a suburb of Los Angeles, and it's right on the ocean. You can roller skate to the beach on paths, and so we decided to go skating. Katie was too young for that, and so she and Dottie went for a walk while the two older children and I strapped on our skates.

As the three of us were skating along, we went by an adobe wall covered with graffiti, and every bit of it was vulgar. All the words you can think of were there. My kids, ages eight and ten, looked at that and started whispering to each other.

I saw it for the opportunity it was. I said to Kelly and Sean, "Let's go get a Coke." We went and got our soft drinks, and then we came back and sat down right in front of that wall. The three of us with our skates sticking out were staring at all that foul mess. I said, "Children, may I explain this to you?"

Naturally they were eager to hear what I would say, and so I started with the various four-letter words and explained again just what they meant. Then I explained the other words and pictures—everything on the wall. The kids were all eyes and ears. I explained how these words and gestures distorted and cheapened one of the most beautiful gifts God has given to a husband and wife.

Next I explained to them how what people say and do reflects their character. I asked, "Children, can I tell you why I get very upset when I hear people use four-letter words with a sexual connotation to put people down?"

"Sure, Dad," they responded.

"Your dad is a communicator, kids, mainly in high schools and universities. I'll be in a fraternity talking to some guys about sex, nailing them right where they sleep. And do you know how they try to justify their involvement in premarital sex?"

"How, Dad?"

"They'll say, 'Oh, come on, Josh. Sex is so beautiful, so wonderful, so meaningful. It's love.' And sometimes they almost convince me they mean it."

"They don't?" Sean asked.

"No, they don't. Those same students will walk out of there, and as soon as they want to put someone down or degrade them, they'll use four-letter words or vulgar gestures with sexual connotations to emphasize their point. Now, children, if sex is so beautiful and meaningful to them, if to them it is an expression of love, why would they use vulgar sexual language when they want to degrade someone? Remember one thing Jesus taught in Matthew 15:11: it's not what goes into a person that defiles him but what comes out."

When I had explained how words and actions reflect character, I said, "Children, as a father who loves you and wants to protect and provide for you so that you can have all your mom and I have in marriage, I want to encourage you to never date people who use vulgar language with sexual connotations. And I beg you never to marry someone who talks that way; *because if you do, you're going to be the object of their vulgar sexual attitude every time you make love to that person.*"

Kelly and Sean have never forgotten that day, either. About three years later, Kelly and I were in a yogurt shop one day when some high school kids walked in. Their language was full of sexually connotated four-letter words. Kelly, who was then twelve, turned to me and said, "Daddy, that's not right, is it?"

I said, "No, but why isn't it?"

She then related to me our entire conversation that day on the beach at Venice. The lesson had really stuck. And you can do the same kind of teaching if you just look for the opportunities. Let the explanations and understanding come from you as a parent. You can put sex in the right perspective. You can share God's purpose of sex, its beauty, and how that many people today are very distant from God's original design.

Bear in mind as you teach that each child is unique. Some kids will be able to understand more at an earlier age than others. Some will ask more questions. Some will just think a little differently. Be sensitive to your child's ability to understand, to his or her level of interest, and to the most effective ways for him or her to learn. Don't make the mistake of trying to push every child into one mold.

The Importance of the Parents' Relationship

Your relationship with your spouse is another important element in the sex education of your children. I've talked about how sex should be presented as a normal, healthy part of life, and about how we need to discuss it frankly, using the correct terms without embarrassment. It's difficult to do that, however, unless it's the way we feel about sex ourselves. If we're embarrassed to talk about it, that feeling is bound to come through to our children. Often the uneasiness comes from our own family background.

Take some time, then, to examine your own feelings about sex. Do you enjoy it? Are you comfortable discussing it with your spouse? Are you able to tell each other what you do and don't like? If there are problems in your own sexual life, you need to make some progress in those areas before you can give your child a healthy perspective on the subject.

About Sex Ed in School

Although it is not my purpose in this book to say much about sex education in the schools, I feel I do need to address the subject briefly. Let me begin by saying that regardless of what's taught in the schools, the primary responsibility for our children's sex education belongs to us, the parents. And that education should begin long before our children enter school.

Having said that, let me make three points about sex education in the schools. *First,* you should look carefully at what's being taught in your child's school and then reach your own conclusions about it. You have that right as a parent. If you don't like what you see, talk to the teacher or principal. But whether you end up liking what you see or not, take the time and effort to check it out.

Second, whatever is being taught in your child's school, continue your education efforts at home. Don't let the school take your place in teaching and instilling values in this vital area. Review the school material with your child if your child feels comfortable with it; this will probably become more difficult as your child enters adolescence. At the very least, maintain the kind of open communication where your child will feel free to ask questions about what he's been taught in the classroom. The key to maintaining open communication, again, will be the kind of relationship you've built over the years.

And *third,* as you evaluate what others are teaching your child, understand that there's no such thing as value-neutral sex education. Much of the material being used in public schools today purports to be value-neutral, concentrating on the biological aspects of sex. The fact is, however, that *any* material on such a subject *inevitably* teaches one set of values or another, even if it's not intentional.

Suppose, for example, that some material were actually as free of any moral values as it's humanly possible to make it, talking only about the biological facts of sex and reproduction. What values message would that material convey to children? None? Think again. It would be saying by implication that sex is only a biological act, nothing more. It would imply by omission that love, caring, and, most importantly, the commitment of marriage are unnecessary to an adequate discussion of sexuality. And that implication just isn't true.

U. S. Secretary of Education William Bennett put the whole matter very succinctly: "Studies show that when parents are the main source of sex education, children are less likely to engage in sex. This should come as no surprise when one remembers that the home is the crucible of character, and that parents are children's first and foremost teachers."

Sociologist Brent Miller did a study at Utah State University on more than 1,000 teenagers to find the effects of parents' teaching sex education to their children. He discovered that the more openly parents talked to teens about sex-related values and beliefs, the less active their children were in sexual behavior. Another interesting discovery was that if the teens learned the sexual facts from their own parents, they were significantly less likely to become sexually active than those teenagers who learned the facts about sex from their friends.

TRY IT YOURSELF
Ideas for Providing Sound Sex Education

For young children

1. Buy *Almost Twelve* by Ken Taylor and work through it with your child. It may seem as if it is too early to teach this information, but you need to communicate it not at "twelve," but by six or seven.

2. Use Dr. James Dobson's "Preparing for Adolescence" audiocassette series. Take your child on a weekend trip and listen to it together.

For older children

1. Discuss with your teenager these eight facts that research has established concerning the probable effect of premarital intercourse:

   a. Premarital sex tends to break up couples.

   b. Many men do not want to marry a woman who has had intercourse with someone else.

   c. Those who have premarital sex tend to have less happy marriages.

d. Those who have premarital sex are more likely to have their marriage end in divorce.

e. Persons and couples who have had premarital sex are more likely to have extramarital affairs as well.

f. Having premarital sex frequently leads a person into marrying an individual not well-suited to her or him.

g. Persons and couples with premarital sex experience seem to achieve sexual satisfaction sooner after marriage, *but . . .*

h. They are likely to be less satisfied overall with their sex life during marriage.

For many more positive reasons to wait see the resource book, *Why Wait?*

Recommended Reading

How to Teach Your Child about Sex by Grace Ketterman (Old Tappan, NJ: Fleming H. Revell, 1981)

Talking Together about Love and Sexuality by Mildred Tengbom (Minneapolis: Bethany House, 1985)

A Parent's Guide to Sex Education by Mary Ann Mayo (Grand Rapids: Zondervan, 1986)

Sex Education Is for the Family by Tim LaHaye (Grand Rapids: Zondervan, 1985)

Almost Twelve by Ken Taylor (Wheaton: Tyndale, 1968)

Preparing for Adolescence by James Dobson (New York: Bantam, 1980)

Why Wait? by Josh McDowell (San Bernardino: Here's Life Publishers, 1987)

12 ♂

How to Set Dating Standards

A GOOD-NIGHT KISS that put me on cloud nine during our first month of dating turned into hours of passionate kissing in front of his fireplace. I started to innocently justify staying at his house on occasion, due to the half hour drive home. I was slipping, making small allowances for further advance in our relationship.

Oh, I knew it wasn't right, and I knew it wasn't the relationship that God would want for me, yet I wasn't strong enough to end it. I felt apathetic toward God, and I didn't feel like saying no to Rick. Compromise had weakened me. By the time we had intercourse, it was so easy to let down the final defense.

Here was a Christian young woman who loved the Lord, yet one bad decision started her down a road toward moral compromise. Her story tragically illustrates how vital it is for young people to set and stick to standards in dating and relationship-building. In this chapter, we are going to look at how you can help your child do just that.

By the time your child begins dating, I trust he or she will be a Christian whose life is dedicated to serving and walking with God. If that's true—and I'm going to assume it is through the rest of this chapter—then the bottom line on dating should be exactly the same as the bottom line on every other part of your child's life. His or her goal should be to please and honor God in dating relationships and practices. just as in everything else.

If your child is not walking closely with the Lord, however, you should still guide him or her in setting standards for dating relationships. You can appeal to whatever relationship he or she has with the Lord or to his or her own conscience. And if you can't build your discussion of dating standards on the teen's relationship with the Lord, then build it on the teen's relationship with you. While your first priority ought to be to lead your teenager into a close walk with the Lord, until that happens, continue to work with him or her on standards for dating.

As you prepare your child for dating, instill in his or her mind the truth that God really does want what's best for his child, and that following guidelines that will honor the Lord is actually in his or her own best interest. That's the foundation on which a healthy dating life can be built. It would be helpful as a parent for you to see the section on positive reasons to wait in my book, *Why Wait?* It will greatly help you to explain the benefits of waiting to your child.

Whom Should They Date?

One of the principle standards for dating relationships you will want to instill in your child is this—namely, that he or she will not date a non-Christian. The complete text of the biblical injunction that applies here is this: "Do not be unequally yoked together with unbelievers. For what fellowship has righteousness with lawlessness? And what communion has light with darkness?" (2 Cor. 6:14).

The simple fact is that for Christians it is a delicate matter to date non-Christians. *First,* everyone a person dates is, however remotely, a possible candidate for marriage. And there's no question but that a believer should never marry an unbeliever. Since if a person gets married it will be to someone he has dated, it only makes sense that the people one dates should meet at least the most basic requirement of a marriage partner—that of being a Christian.

Second, even if there is no intention of marriage, a non-Christian doesn't share a Christian's convictions and standards. There are moral non-Christians, to be sure, but even with the best intentions, dating non-Christians can lead to the kind of immorality in which the young woman at the beginning of the chapter became involved. It's a significant dilemma for the Christian teen that can best be handled by avoiding the situation altogether by not dating non-Christians.

Not only should the people our children date be Christians, but they should be people with the same convictions. The people our children date should have the same understanding of the importance of serving and walking with God and living according to His standards. Our children's dates will be much more fun—and safer—if the people they date are spiritually compatible.

Now, even if your child acknowledges the wisdom of dating only those who share the same Christian commitment and convictions, that doesn't guarantee it will be easy to keep this agreement. In the first place, it may seem or actually be difficult to find other young people who share these convictions. I've had a number of Christian teens say to me, "I just don't know many kids who have the same perspective, and I'm not interested in dating the girls (or boys) I do know."

This can be a serious problem for an adolescent who feels ready to date. As parents, we can help by getting our children involved with as many different Christian kids as possible. When children approach this age, it's important for them to be in a church with a good-sized and active youth group, if at all possible.

If your church's youth group is small, perhaps it can do some things jointly with other nearby church groups. If your church has no youth group at all, encourage your child to participate in another church's youth program. The leaders of that other church will likely be very understanding of your child's need and welcome him or her.

Finally, in helping your child determine whom to date, teach him or her by example and by instruction to go below the surface in evaluating people. The adolescent world focuses on three things in judging the desirability of a potential date: looks, personality, and popularity. But looks and popularity are extremely superficial and don't really say anything about a person, and even personality doesn't reveal much about such important inner qualities as character and convictions.

If our children can accept and hold that perspective, the field of potential dates might expand a good deal. And they might make some friends of the opposite sex that they otherwise would have never come to know.

What Should Be the Standards?

When your children are ready to date, it's vital to have standards in place before they go out for the first time. These standards, based on their own convictions, should guide them in determining where they go and what they do. Without such standards, a young person starting to date feels adrift in a sea of uncertainty about what to do and what is and isn't acceptable. But with such standards, a young person can begin dating with the confidence of knowing what should happen in his dating life.

Let me emphasize that the standards we're talking about must be the child's own standards based on his or her own convictions—not our standards based on our convictions and forced upon our children. Our role as parents is that of teacher and encourager, not dictator.

Although your child's standards for dating must be his own, you, the parent, must take the initiative when it comes to getting these standards created. Talk with your child about the value and benefits of having such a set of standards. Discuss what those standards should be, and have your child write them down as agreement is reached on each one of them. You should certainly have input, but the final decisions in most areas ought to be left with your child.

You can lay down some ground rules like curfews, but even there the specifics should be negotiated. That way, even if you and your child can't reach agreement and you have to impose a decision, your child will at least know that his or her thoughts were given a fair hearing. Even adolescents still have some appreciation for boundaries, recognizing instinctively that boundaries demonstrate your love as a parent. But again, your goal as a parent is to rear a child who is more and more *self*-directed as he or she approaches adulthood.

It is to be hoped that your child will agree that setting some standards and writing them out before dating begins is a good idea. But what are some of the specific standards that you will want to recommend to your child in addition to the matter of whom he or she will date?

First, your child should write out some goals for dating. Why does he or she want to date? What does he or she hope to have happen? Obviously, having fun is a major goal, as is getting to know the other person. But encourage your child also to think in terms of serving the other person and honoring God. If these qualities are a part of his or her goals, he or she will have more enjoyable dates and will be less likely to slide into sexual activity as well.

Second, suggest that each date should begin with a brief prayer in which your child and his friend commit that time together to the Lord. This may sound strange and awkward, but if your child is dating people who share his or her Christian convictions, it shouldn't be so difficult. It will set the right tone for a date and get it off to a good start. It will remind them both of their individual relationships with God, and of His presence with them during the date, too.

Third, a first date should always involve activity that will provide good opportunity for conversation, since that is the best way to get to know someone. A movie or a concert does not provide such an opportunity. Playing Frisbee or riding bikes in the park does. A first date in which two people can talk together at length gives them a chance to explore common interests and tastes, how their senses of humor compare, and other areas of personality and character.

If your child has trouble thinking of good date ideas that provide the opportunity for discussion, or if he doesn't know how to carry on an interesting and enjoyable conversation, ask if you can help him. Some ideas are found in the "Try It Yourself" section at the end of this chapter. Others are found in a wonderfully helpful book, *Dynamic Dating,* by Barry St. Clair and William H. Jones (Here's Life Publishers, 1987) and in my own book, *Givers, Takers, and Other Kinds of Lovers* (Here's Life Publishers, 1981).

Fourth, no young person (or any person, for that matter) should assume he or she is strong enough to handle temptation and thus put himself or herself in temptation's way. Rather, the assumption should be that we are all capable of sinning, and therefore the plan for a date should specifically avoid places and circumstances where temptation to immorality is likely. This might include parties where drugs or alcohol will be available, R- or X-rated movies, or time spent in your child's or the date's home if the parents are not there.

It is also wise for young people on a date to avoid being alone together. Dates should take place in public places or with other family members. Group dating with other like-minded young people should also be encouraged.

Fifth, dates should intentionally focus on aspects of the relationship other than the physical. Your child and his or her date should seek to develop a friendship such that when they stop dating each other, they will still respect each other and consider themselves lasting friends. This means that they should get to know one another intellectually, emotionally, and spiritually.

Finally, the big question is that of standards in the physical aspect of dating. Is holding hands okay? Is kissing okay? How about petting? Just how far is too far? I hope you won't think I'm ducking the question when I say that it's difficult if not impossible for me to answer with specific, hard-and-fast rules that apply equally to everyone. Much depends on your unique child and the person he or she is dating, as well as on your feelings as a family. It also depends on the emotional and spiritual maturity of your child and his or her date.

However, some general biblical guidelines ought to be the foundation for any specific standards on which you and your child may agree. First and foremost, of course, is that in this area as in all other aspects of life, the primary motivation should be to honor and please God. Thus, if a young person wants to know how much he can "get away with" before he crosses some line and God zaps him, his whole perspective is wrong. He should be thinking, instead, *Would God be pleased or disappointed by what I am contemplating doing?*

Am I saying there should never be any physical contact? We were made by God to need and enjoy physical contact. And God is not a prude. In the right setting and kept under control, young people can enjoy holding hands, a quick hug, or a light kiss. You, however, need to decide this with your child. Although I can't say there should never be any physical contact, it is safest and appropriate for your teen to have as a principle of dating that he or she avoid it.

One more way to put this to your child is to say, "Don't light a fire that you can't put out." In other words, don't create arousal that you can't satisfy in a God-honoring way. Sexual arousal is meant to lead to sexual intercourse, and once that fire starts to burn, it can quickly turn into a wildfire that is extremely difficult to get under control. Some couples can hold hands and kiss a little without losing control, but others will need pretty much to abstain from even light kissing. Again, much depends on your particular child and the individual he or she is dating.

The perspective your child needs to keep in mind is that the person he or she is dating is a friend whom he or she respects, and not to be manipulated for one's own pleasure. You might also suggest that your child think in terms of treating his dates just the way he hopes someone else that night is treating the person he will eventually marry. In addition, your teen should remember that his or her date is someone else's future husband or wife.

When Should They Start Dating?

Another big question we parents face is when to let our children start dating. Many adolescents begin quite young, as early as eleven or twelve years of age. But just because "everybody else is dating" (which they are not at eleven or twelve) is no reason to let your child date then. You need to do what's best for your child.

Here again, however, there are no hard and fast rules. There's no one age that's right for every boy or girl to begin dating. Each child is unique, and so each child will be ready in his own time. How do you tell when that time has come?

The time to date has come when you as the parent are confident that your child is mature enough to date responsibly. That means your child is ready to set some standards along the lines we've discussed and *stick to them*. If your child isn't ready for that, he or she is not ready to say no to the pressures toward premarital sexual involvement. And such a child should certainly not be out dating.

Only you can determine when your child is ready to date. Once you've given the green light, the standards have to be worked out with your child. But you are the only one (with your spouse) who should give the go ahead. And you should be confident when you do so—through conversation, through observation, and through your child's acting responsibly in other areas of life—that your child will set standards consistent with the family's Christian values and convictions.

I want to caution you to be extremely reluctant to let even a child who seems mature start dating early. Adolescents mature quickly, and each year that a child waits will help him be better prepared for the experience. Statistics bear this out clearly. Research shows that 91 percent of all girls who start dating at age twelve have had sex before graduation from high school. This is true of only 56 percent of those who start dating at thirteen, of 53 percent of those who begin at fourteen, of 40 percent of those who start at fifteen, and only 20 percent of those who begin dating at age sixteen. So be cautious in deciding when to let your child begin. It's better by far to err on the side of making your child wait a little longer than may be necessary.

In the next chapter, we'll look at arming our children with reasons to say no to sexual pressure if, in spite of efforts to avoid it, he or she finds himself or herself faced with temptation to have intercourse.

TRY IT YOURSELF
Ideas for Setting Standards for Relationship Building and Dating

I mentioned earlier the book *Dynamic Dating* by Barry St. Clair and William H. Jones. It is written to teenagers and includes a very helpful guide for setting standards for relationship building and dating. Here are some of the many practical suggestions in the book.

What can your teenager do on a date? The number of ideas is almost infinite. He or she should rarely have to do the same thing twice. Planning is the key. Encourage your teenager to use these steps as he plans his date: 1) think creatively, 2) choose from different types of dates depending on the occasion, mood, and personal preference of his date.

Sports dates:

golf	basketball	tennis
miniature golf	croquet	racquetball
badminton	horseshoes	bowling
pool/bumper pool	walking	roller skating
ice skating	waterskiing	jogging
swimming	ping pong	Frisbee

Sports dates are fun, good exercise, can involve others, and are usually inexpensive. However, your date might not be interested in sports, your date could hurt your ego by beating you, you could get too competitive, or your date could get injured. An idea for a sports date is to have your date ride her bicycle while you run. Afterward, go for something to drink while you cool down.

Outdoor dates:

boating	canoeing	sailing
rafting	sightseeing	hiking
fishing	mountain climbing	bicycling
horseback riding	going on a picnic	building a sand castle
visiting an amusement park	visiting an outdoor garden	visiting a wildlife sanctuary
visiting a zoo	visiting a state park	taking a drive in the country
watching a sunrise or sunset	collecting seashells	having a cookout
	flying kites	playing shuffleboard

Crazy dates:

go to a fair	go for a hay ride	make a video
go on a double date with parents	go on a group date in a convertible	go for an airplane ride
have a water pistol fight	have a water balloon fight	learn to drive a stick shift
dress up like the '50s and get your picture taken	have a scavenger hunt with a polaroid camera or a tape recorder (have two couples think up items for one another to look for)	
plant a garden		

The advantages of crazy dates are that they are memorable, creative, fun, and can involve others. The disadvantages are the potential that the date can be a flop and that some people might think you are weird.

There are many more ideas in *Dynamic Dating,* a book directed at your teenager. I would highly recommend it for you as a parent to better relate to your own children.

[This material is taken from *Dynamic Dating* by Barry St. Clair and William H. Jones, Here's Life Publishers, 1987, and used by permission.]

Further resources: Givers, Takers and Other Kinds of Lovers and *Dating: Picking (and Being) a Winner.*

13 ♂

How to Equip Them with Reasons to Wait

MY LIFE IS DEDICATED to being a Christian apologist. I believe that when people are asked to make a major commitment such as to become a Christian, they deserve some compelling reasons for that decision. They deserve evidence to demonstrate that what is being asked of them makes sense and can be defended. When people become Christians, they don't have to leave their minds at the door.

The same thing is true when we tell our kids to say no to premarital sex. They don't have to go along with us just because we are their parents or "just because the Bible says so." There are sound, compelling reasons that any young person with a mind even halfway open will recognize as valid.

Tragically, our society doesn't give kids reasons to say no. Just the reverse is true. It actively encourages them to jump into bed with others, and it tries to minimize or hide altogether the painful consequences.

Consider, for example, that just a few years ago we would hear occasionally about venereal diseases. Everyone knew that venereal diseases were picked up by being sexually promiscuous. There was a definite stigma attached to such conditions. But have you noticed how you rarely hear the term *venereal disease* any more?

The description in vogue now is "sexually transmitted

diseases," which doesn't have the same stigma associated with it. These are diseases that any ordinary person supposedly gets now—they just happen to be sexually transmitted. And as if that didn't do enough to obscure things, more and more we're hearing just the initials, STDs, which even further diminishes the impact of what's going on. Our society, which accepts and even promotes sexual promiscuity, is trying to make these diseases just another public health concern without relating them to a very real moral issue.

When it comes to our adolescent children, they are being bombarded with the message that sex is great whenever you can get it, and that waiting for marriage is incredibly old-fashioned. I've had many kids tell me that they have had all kinds of pressure to get involved in sex, and that no one had ever given them any good reasons to say no.

That young people have not been told the many valid reasons to say no to premarital sex is tragic. This chapter contains some of these reasons. You can pass them on to your child in the kind of informal teaching situation we've discussed in earlier chapters. For an extensive treatment of these and other reasons to say no, refer to my book, *Why Wait?* (Here's Life Publishers, 1987).

Place "No" in the Positive

Any discussion of reasons for saying no to premarital sex must begin with an understanding of the character of God. I've talked about this several times already, but it bears repeating again. God is not a cosmic killjoy bent on ruining any fun His human creatures might try to have. He didn't make us to enjoy sex only to frustrate us by severely limiting when and with whom it's okay to experience that pleasure. Nor is He arbitrary and capricious. Just the opposite is true.

God designed us and made us. He is all-knowing and loves us so much that He sent His Son to die for us. Consequently, He knows what is best for us, and everything He

rdains for us is meant for our best good. In Deuteronomy
0:13, Moses implored the people of Israel "to keep the com-
mandments of the Lord and His statutes which I command
ou today *for your good*" (emphasis added).

Psalm 84:11 speaks in a similar vein: "The Lord will give
race and glory; no good thing will He withhold from those
who walk uprightly." And James 1:17 tells us, "Every good gift
nd every perfect gift is from above and comes down from the
Father of lights, with whom there is no variation or shadow of
urning."

God knows and wants what's best for us. He knows how
he human spirit, mind, and body work, and how human relationships function most joyfully. So when He says sex belongs
only in the marriage bed, He isn't restricting our fun; He's
howing us the way to enjoy it best. God is not trying to keep us
rom having a wonderful sex life; He's giving us positive in-
truction in how to have the most wonderful sex life possible.

Unfortunately, even Christians are ignorant of this per-
pective, or else we forget. We tend to think of God's commands
s being only negatives designed to frustrate any enjoyment we
might get out of life. It is true that many of God's commands are
ouched in negative language, but they are given to us for positive reasons. To tell a child not to touch a hot stove is not being
negative and keeping him from having fun; it is being positive
by keeping him from harm. If he burned himself, it would prevent him from enjoying life for a while.

Whenever God gives a command, there are at least two
positive reasons behind it. First, He's trying to *protect* us from
ome harm. And second, He's trying to *provide* something good
for us. As we look at reasons for saying no to premarital sex,
we'll be considering both of these aspects of why our children
would do well to abstain.

Suppose a world-class hurdler like Greg Foster or Renaldo
Nehemiah trained hard and sacrificially for four years to prepare for the Olympics. But when he showed up for the race,
he found there were no lanes marked to keep the runners from

crashing into each other. What if the hurdles were scattered al
over the track and there was no finish line to designate the enc
of the race?

The resulting race would be a dangerous chaos, with runners banging into each other, cutting one another with thei
spikes, tripping over each other and the hurdles, and running
around in confusion as they tried to figure out how and where
the race was to end.

In much the same way as an Olympic race needs to be se
up and managed by someone who knows what he is doing, we
need the One who knows what He's doing and how this life is to
be lived to set the boundaries for us. Fortunately, God ha:
done so even before we asked, primarily in His Word, the
Bible.

Physical Reasons to Wait

There are solid reasons to say no to premarital sex in four
major areas: physical, spiritual, emotional, and relational. We
will look at each of these in turn.

In the physical realm, God wants, first, to protect us from
addiction to premarital sex. Sex is an extremely pleasurable
activity, and it's very possible to get hooked on it. Many kids
do. Said one young person, "I won't try to pretend passionate
physical exchange isn't enjoyable. But I do want to say that
outside of marriage, the enjoyment is short-lived. And when it
is over you are left disappointed, looking for another fix to
appease your lust, much like a drug addict craves another hit."

Illicit sex can become a real addiction causing all kinds of
grief, and our loving Lord wants to protect you and me and our
children from that.

Second, God wants to protect our young people from the
way premarital sex can damage their self-image by putting
them on a performance basis. In the insecurity of a premarital
relationship which involves sexual intercourse, one or both of
the people is continually going to be anxious about his or her
performance, knowing that as soon as his ability to please the

other person sexually diminishes, the relationship is in deep trouble.

Debora Phillips, author of *Sexual Confidence* and director of the Princeton Center for Behavior Therapy, wrote, "Due to the instant sex of the sexual revolution, people perform rather than make love. Many women can't achieve a sense of intimacy, and their anxiety about how well they perform blocks their chances for honest arousal. Without genuine involvement, they haven't much chance for courtship, romance or love. They're left feeling cheated and burned out."

Third, God wants to protect our children from the threat of sexually transmitted diseases, which, as I pointed out at the beginning of this book, are reaching epidemic proportions. The Minnesota Institute of Public Health warns that "there are twenty sexually transmitted diseases which are not prevented by contraception." It further points out that fifteen million people now contract a sexual disease each year. In one sexual encounter, it is possible to pick up as many as five separate diseases.

Anyone who has sex outside of marriage is at risk. As one researcher put it, "Unless you're monogamous for a lifetime, with a monogamous partner, you're at risk. And the more partners you have, the greater the risk."

AIDS is the deadliest of these diseases and the one getting the most publicity, but it is hardly the only one. Chlamydia, genital herpes, gonorrhea, trichomoniasis, syphilis, and pelvic-inflammatory disease (PID) are just a few of the many sexually transmitted illnesses running rampant today—many with no cure.

One non-Christian young man said to me after I had spoken once in San Diego, "I've had a real free-love lifestyle—casual relationships, meaningful relationships, plenty of sex. Then herpes came onto the scene. It got my attention, but it didn't change my lifestyle because it's not fatal. You can never get rid of it, but it's not fatal. Then AIDS came onto the scene, and I decided I had to change my lifestyle. So I found a woman I cared about, fell in love, got married, and she gave me herpes."

God doesn't want anything like that to happen to our children.

Fourth, God wants to protect our children from unwanted pregnancy and abortion. As one teen said, "When you are a teenager and you become pregnant, you have several options open to you, none of them favorable."

There is no perfect contraceptive, no 100 percent foolproof way of preventing pregnancy other than abstinence. As another teenager put it, "I wonder about the pregnant girls I see at school. What are they feeling? What are their desires, hurts, frustrations? What will their lives be like? And aside from the obvious biological aspect, *why are they pregnant?* If two people don't have the love needed to raise a family (which, if they did, they would be married), they have no business taking the chance of getting pregnant outside of marriage."

To protect our children from the physical dangers it brings, God says not to engage in premarital intercourse. On the positive side, physically, God wants to provide our children the full beauty of sexual oneness in marriage. Within the security, love, and commitment of marriage, sex can reach its fullest and most exciting potential.

The Lord wants two people to enter marriage free from guilt and emotional scars, free from past experiences to which the marriage partner will always be compared, free to be fully one with a lifetime mate. He knows that this is the only way to experience maximum sex, and that's what He wants for us— nothing less.

Spiritual Reasons to Wait

From the spiritual perspective, God wants first to protect our children from sinning against their own bodies and losing respect for themselves and their bodies. First Corinthians 6:18 says, "Flee sexual immorality. Every sin that a man does is outside the body, but he who commits sexual immorality sins against his own body."

When a young person engages in premarital sex, however,

there is often a deep loss of respect not only for his or her own body, but also for the body of the partner. And when that respect is gone, it becomes much easier for a person to become truly promiscuous. The Lord doesn't want this to happen to our children.

Second, God wants to protect our kids from His righteous judgment. "Marriage is honorable among all, and the bed undefiled; but fornicators and adulterers God will judge" (Heb. 13:4). Paul wrote in 1 Thessalonians 4:8 that God will judge sexual immorality. God is holy, and He must judge those who violate His commands. David's sin with Bathsheba as recorded in 2 Samuel 11-12 is a perfect example of this. Out of their adultery, a child was born, and in judgment God took that child's life. It was a painful judgment for David, but God could not tolerate what had happened.

The Lord's judgment isn't always as swift as it was in the case of David and Bathsheba, but it is always sure. Those who engage in premarital sex are subject to that judgment sooner or later, but those who stay pure need have no fear on that account. And God wants our children to be safe from such reckoning with His justice.

Third, God wants to protect our children from anything that will tend to break their fellowship with Him. It's hard to be comfortable with someone who makes you feel guilty just by his presence, and when a young person is engaged in ongoing premarital sex, there's a lot of guilt. In such cases, God is uncomfortable to be around, and so the young person withdraws from Him.

The *final* spiritual reason to say no to premarital sex is that God wants to protect our children from being poor witnesses to non-Christians because of sinful sexual activity. We've seen in earlier chapters that Christian values are different from the world's, and that consequently there should be a noticeable difference in lifestyles. But if that difference isn't there, if the Christian adolescent is as sexually active as other kids, what will attract the unsaved to Christ? What will make them see that their lives need to be changed by God?

It was specifically because of the damage to David's godly witness through his sin with Bathsheba that God exercised His judgment against David's child. The prophet Nathan said to David on behalf of the Lord, "Because by this deed you have given great occasion to the enemies of the Lord to blaspheme, the child also who is born to you shall surely die" (2 Sam. 12:14).

It is a serious business with God to be a poor witness to the watching world by deliberate, unrepented sin. We want to protect our children from being guilty of that.

There are positive spiritual reasons to say no to premarital sex. We know that God blesses those who are pure. As we saw earlier in Psalm 84:11, "No good thing will He withhold *from those who walk uprightly*" (emphasis added). In Psalm 34:15 we read, "The eyes of the Lord are on the righteous, And His ears are open to their cry." And in the Sermon on the Mount, Jesus said, "Blessed are the pure in heart, For they shall see God" (Matt. 5:8).

Second, we know that patience—waiting for the right time in God's perfect plan—is one of the fruits of the Spirit as listed in Galatians 5:22-23. Waiting for marriage to have sex develops patience and therefore builds one of the fruits of the Spirit in our children. Patience is part of the supernatural life God has provided for His children if we will only walk in it.

I said earlier that what we've had over the past twenty years is not so much a sexual revolution as a revolution in the search for intimacy. Human beings desperately need intimacy, and in the past that need was met before marriage in families, by one's parents and siblings. With the breakup and insecurity in modern families, however, many young people turn to sexual relationships in the vain hope that they will provide the needed intimacy.

Abstaining from premarital sex, however, allows a child to experience the greatest intimacy any of us can enjoy in a personal relationship with Jesus Christ. In Revelation 3:20 Jesus said, "Look! I have been standing at the door and I am constantly knocking. If anyone hears me calling him and pens the door, I will come in and fellowship with him and he with me" (TLB).

Thus, God does not ask a young person to wait for sex without providing the best kind of intimacy possible to make the wait bearable—a close fellowship with Himself through Jesus Christ. When such a relationship with Christ is developed, love and sexual intimacy with another person will be deeper and more fulfilling. This is because a child won't have to look to the relationship with the other person to meet so many of his or her own needs; many of those needs for security and love will be met in his or her relationship with Jesus Christ. Therefore, in your child's relationship with another person, he or she will be more free to give to the other person and to try to meet the needs of the other person.

Emotional Reasons to Wait

Premarital sex can also cause great emotional stress, and God wants to protect our children from that. Perhaps the biggest problem is the guilt that comes from knowing one has violated God's standards.

As one young person said, "One of the worst feelings many sexually active people experience is to get up the next morning and realize the person lying next to them is a total stranger. This 'morning after' syndrome robs a person of a healthy self-image and a clear conscience, which decreases his ability to experience the transparency needed to cultivate an intimate relationship. On top of that, flashbacks from past sexual encounters can haunt a person the rest of his life, which can leave him feeling 'grimy' in the hands of his current lover."

God doesn't want the minds and consciences of our kids to be plagued by that kind of guilt. The way for them to avoid it is to say no.

In addition to protecting our children from guilt, saying no to premarital sex protects them from misleading feelings. Young people who get involved sexually often confuse sex and love. The powerful emotions at work turn relationships upside down to the point where a person can lose control of his feelings.

When sex and love get confused, so, too, do the concept of giving and taking. Real love always gives and seeks the best interests of the one loved. But in premarital sex, each person is taking for his own reasons. The confusion is compounded by the fact that the taking can sometimes look like giving.

One young person who had engaged in premarital sex wrote to a friend who had also done it, "Looking back, I think you will realize how misguided your feelings were. You thought you were in control of your life because you did what you wanted—you were 'living fast and loose' with no thought to anyone but yourself. You see now it was more like 'selfish control' rather than self-control, and your desire for sex led you into false emotions about your situation. Now there is only depression over your experiences. At the age of 15 you professed your belief in the salvation of Jesus Christ; now, at age 17, you feel lost and empty and you want to die."

Then, too, God wants to protect our children from the way premarital sex can create in them negative feelings about sex. When a young person is sexually active, his or her body comes to associate sex and arousal with the emotions of guilt, resentment over being used, and the fear of getting caught, an unwanted pregnancy, or catching some sexually transmitted disease. This association can grow so strong that it constantly haunts any future sexual relationship, robbing it of pleasure or even preventing arousal.

One young woman said, "I feel physically used and therefore undesirable. My past mistakes are evident on my body. Who would ever want to marry me? Can I ever freely give my body to a man? Would another man even want my body? Can I have children? Do I have some undetected sexually transmitted disease? The past never goes away."

Immoral sex can make the sexual experience seem dirty and tainted to a young person, causing not only hurt feelings now, but tremendous difficulty later in the sexual part of marriage as well. There's only one sure way to avoid that problem—say no.

God also desires to protect our children from the difficulty of breaking off a bad relationship when sex is involved. Sex usually does one of two things to a dating relationship. It either ends a good relationship or it sustains a bad relationship. It sustains a bad relationship because the bonding effect that takes place through sexual intercourse, or even through heavy petting, causes a person to look at the relationship unrealistically. First, those involved believe that the relationship is deeper than it really is. And second, such involvement causes a teen to think that he or she knows the other person better than he really does. And as a result, they don't break off the relationship.

On the positive side emotionally, waiting for marriage to enjoy sex allows maturity to develop. Self-control, character, and the ability to focus more on the true needs of the other person can all grow out of a time of obediently following God's plan.

Waiting also shows love for one's future mate. In essence, a young person who says no is saying, "I value the feelings and respect of my future mate more than the pleasure of the moment." As one young woman put it, "You should give your mate the very best, not put him at the bottom of your list. Your body is a savings account to give to your mate as a wedding present, not to be spent on anything else."

Relational Reasons to Wait

Lastly, God wants our children to wait until marriage for sex to protect them from relational problems. The first of these is a breakdown in communication. One young person said, "Like many others, I have learned that if there is too much touching in a relationship, it can cause uneasy feelings which lead to lack of communication."

Wrote another, "Spending this time on sex takes away

from time which could be spent getting to know each other more. Just at the time when the two need to talk most about their deepening feelings, problems they have, and so on, the verbal communication is stopped."

Second and in the same vein, sex makes a good courtship difficult because, in addition to reducing communication, it usually comes to dominate a premarital relationship. Thus, in the time when a man and woman should really be getting to know each other well and developing the social, intellectual, and emotional aspects of their relationship, that process is cut short by the lack of communication and the focus on the physical.

Third, God wants to protect our children from the comparison of past sexual partners that always plagues people who have engaged in premarital relations. A person who has made love to more than one person will probably never be able to forget former lovers entirely. Thus, even in the marriage bed, such a person will find himself comparing his mate to old partners. This is wrong in and of itself, but it's also unfair to the spouse, because memories get idealized with the passing of time, and so the comparisons aren't even realistic.

The other side of the coin is that if a person knows his or her *spouse* was sexually active before marriage, he or she also knows comparisons are going on in *the spouse's* mind, and he or she will always be nagged by concerns about how he or she compares to the spouse's former lovers. This situation is unhealthy for a marriage, to say the least, and God wants to protect our children from it.

As you can see, there are many valid reasons for our kids to say no to premarital sex. I've just touched the surface of many of those listed here, and there are even more reasons given in my book *Why Wait?* As you share these with your child, he or she should be able to see readily that God's way is best and that God really is acting in love when He commands that sex be enjoyed only within the bonds of marriage.

TRY IT YOURSELF
Ideas for Arming Your Child with Reasons to Say No

1. Find opportunities to share the ideas in this chapter with your child. It is tempting to be dictatorial, but far better to discuss or suggest. "Have your ever considered that . . . ?" is a good way to start. The discussions should be informal. Look for natural opportunities. This will require you to be always alert and ready. Teens are usually more responsive in relaxed, spontaneous situations, and so be on your guard to seize opportunities as they arise.

2. It may sound strange, but a teenager needs to practice ahead of time giving a negative answer to the most common lines used to exert pressure to have sex. Sexual pressure is probably one of the most serious things a teenager is up against and often one of the most powerful. And no one has said it would be easy. Saying no is often more difficult than breaking up the whole relationship, especially knowing that saying yes can keep it together—at least for a while. Also, it's not always easy to cling to one's beliefs under pressure.

In the pages that follow are 24 pressure lines that teens use to get others to be sexually involved. Review these with your child. Much of what you see in these pressure lines is actually emotional blackmail.

Line 1: Everybody's doing it.
Reply: That's great. Then I guess you won't have any problem finding someone else.

Line 2: If you love me, you'll have sex with me.
Reply: If you love me, you'll respect my feelings and not push me into doing something I'm not ready for.
Reply: If you love me, you'll wait.

Line 3: If you won't have sex with me, then I don't want to see you any more.
Reply: Well, if that's the way you feel, I'm going to miss seeing you, but that's the way it's going to be.

Line 4: It's just part of growing up.
Reply: Having sex doesn't mean you are grown up. Being grown up to me means deciding what I believe and then sticking to those beliefs.

Line 5: We had sex once before, so what's the problem now?
Reply: I have a right to change my mind. I've decided to wait.

Line 6: Don't you want to try it to see what it's like?
Reply: What is this? Some kind of commercial ad? Try it; you'll like it! I do plan to try it with my husband (wife).
Line 7: But I have to have it!
Reply: No you don't. If I can wait, you can wait.

Line 8: If you want to be popular with the kids at school, you'll do it.
Reply: I don't have to depend on sex to be popular. I have more to offer than that. People like you because of the kind of person you are and the kind of character you have.

Line 9: You've gotten me all excited. If you love me, you'll prove it.
Reply: Having sex doesn't prove you're in love. I have too much self-respect to get sexually involved before I'm ready for it. I've decided to wait.

Line 10: If you don't, someone else will.
Reply: If all I mean to you is a body to have sex with, maybe we'd better take a closer look at why we see each other. You have no right to use me.

Line 11: If you care about me, you'll have sex with me.
Reply: Because I care about you, I want to wait.
Reply: There are many ways to show someone you care.

Line 12: To love you so much and hold back hurts!
Reply: Love is worth some sacrifice.

Line 13: Sex will cause our love to grow.
Reply: Yes, but into what?

Line 14: I can really turn you on.
Reply: The only thing that needs to be turned on in here are the lights.

Line 15: Want to go upstairs and check out my new waterbed?
Reply: Nope—I don't swim.

Line 16: You just don't know what you're missing.
Reply: That will make two of us. You won't know what you're missing either.

Line 17: Want to go to bed?
Reply: No, thanks. I just got up.

Line 18: You don't want people to think you're not a man (woman), do you?
Reply: Having sex doesn't prove a person is a man (woman). My dog has sex and he's not a man.

Line 19: Don't worry. I'll use protection.
Reply: You're going to need protection if you don't leave me alone.

Line 20: Would you like to get in the back seat?
Reply: No, I'd rather sit up here with you.

Line 21: I do it with all my girlfriends.
Reply: Well, I guess I won't be your girlfriend.

Line 22: Kissing turns me on, and it's not enough.
Reply: Well, it's enough for me.

Line 23: You mean you're still a virgin? What are you, frigid?
Reply: No, I'm smart.

Line 24: Sex makes you have a good complexion.
Reply: I'd rather use make-up then.

Further resources: Why Wait? (pp. 307–415).

14 ♂

We Can Win the Battle

THERE'S A BATTLE RAGING today for the bodies and souls of America's teenagers, and like it or not, our children are on the front line. Venereal diseases, unwanted pregnancies, guilt, loss of self-esteem, and breakdown in relationships are just some of the results of premarital sexual involvement.

My desire for you as a parent is that you never hear the following statements; or, if you do, that you might know what to do when you hear them.

> If only I had waited. I see now how uncluttered my life would have been, how my mind would have been free from this burden that besets me even years later.
>
> If you want to know what it is really like, get two pieces of paper and glue part of one to the other. After it has dried, pull them apart. What you have in your hand is a vivid picture of two people after a premarital sexual relationship—both torn, both leaving a part of themselves with the other.
>
> All my relationships had two things in common: one was we made love a lot, and the other was that they always ended and I always went through (and am still going through) incredible pain. I don't know if the break-ups were because God didn't want us having sex or

141

because of other reasons, but they hurt worse than anything ever has.

I finally got a girl into bed (actually it was in a car) when I was seventeen. I thought I was the hottest thing there was, but then she started saying she loved me and started getting clingy. I figured out that there had probably been a dozen guys before me who thought they had "conquered" her, but who were really just objects of her need for security. This took all the wind out of my sails. Worse yet, I couldn't respect someone who gave in as easy as she did, and I was amazed to find that after four weeks of sex as often as I wanted, I was tired of her. I didn't see any point in continuing the relationship. I finally dumped her, which made me feel even worse, because even I could see she was hurting. At least one of her parents was an alcoholic (maybe both were) and her home life was a disaster, and just when she thought she could hold on to someone, I ditched her. I didn't feel very cool after that. I felt pretty low.

I gave no thought to what I would tell my future wife about those months when my girlfriend and I engaged in all the pleasures of the marriage bed with none of the commitment. A wife was a nebulous figure in the far-off future, not a person with feelings or someone who would care that I had been intimate with anyone besides her.

You CAN Make the Difference

Please don't conclude, however, that the struggle to protect your child from all this is hopeless. Far from it! There is no doubt that we as parents have a tremendous influence on our children whatever their age, and we can do a great deal to help them say no to the pressures they are facing today to get involved in premarital sex.

My perspective as a father is that this is a battle my family can win, and I'm going to do everything in my power to make that happen. Not only that, but we are going to have a lot of fun along the way.

Helping our children say no to premarital sex begins by understanding what it's like to be an adolescent today. Try to look at things from your child's point of view—the onset of puberty; the hormones going crazy; the message about sex in movies, music, television, and everywhere else he or she turns; the peer pressure; the need for intimacy and the insecurity of family life; the misinformation about sex; and the lack of good role models. If you think being a parent is tough these days, try being an adolescent!

Along with that, understand why kids say yes to premarital sex. Go back and read chapter 4 if you need to. Kids say yes for many reasons and not just because they are wild or rebellious.

Next, develop and maintain the attitude that you can help your child, that regardless of his age, you can make a positive difference in his other life. Never allow a rough period of time in the relationship to take away your confidence that you can win. And while I haven't made a point of saying it before, since it is so basic that I have assumed you would do it anyway, bathe your efforts as a parent in prayer daily. When our strength and wisdom fail, His are more than sufficient.

If you are married, work on your relationship with your spouse. That is so important because out of your daily interaction needs to come the security your child needs—the model of how to love, and the model of how to enjoy sex in the proper context.

Then build a relationship with your child that conveys to him or her your unconditional acceptance, appreciation, availability, affection, and accountability. This relationship is what earns you the right to teach your child the truths and values on which you want him to build his life. Remember that rules without relationship equal rebellion. There's no substitute for a strong relationship with your child; I can't emphasize this too heavily.

Teach your child to think for himself or herself and not just go along with the crowd, and teach him to think Christianly. Help him to think of the consequences of his words and actions, and not merely what seems fun at the moment. By your example and through discussion, teach him to view every decision in terms of whether a particular choice would honor God and help to build his relationship with the Savior.

Surround your child with a healthy circle of contacts: friends, teachers, coaches, and other family members if they are nearby. Find places where your child will be exposed to positive peer pressure as well as good adult role models.

Take advantage of natural opportunities to teach your child about sex—the whole truth. Give him not only the biological facts, but also God's perfect plan for sex. Help him to see that the sexual relationship creates a oneness which is much more than physical, and that this oneness can only be healthy and beautiful within the lifelong commitment of marriage.

Carefully determine when your child is ready to start dating based on his or her demonstrated level of maturity. And when he or she is ready, help develop standards for dating that will honor God, that will protect the young person, and that will help him or her enjoy real fun which carries no guilt with it.

Arm your child with the "evidence" as well as biblical reasons to say no to sex. Don't let him or her be the victim of ignorance, and don't let him or her be defenseless in the face of pressure.

Finally, build into your relationship with your child an atmosphere of forgiveness. Make your home a place that, like the prodigal child's home, your child will want to return to if he or she fails. Model always the love and forgiveness of our loving heavenly Father. One of the most significant things you can do to help your child say no to sex—or to any other temptation—is to build a strong relationship with him or her in which your unconditional love and acceptance is clearly realized by your child.

You can win the battle. It is worth developing a fantastic relationship with your child. It is not easy and it doesn't come naturally—I know I have to work hard at it every day. But parenting can be just about the most exciting part of your life. That's what God wants for you, and it is my prayer for you, too.

P.S. I have included an appendix that is from a real-life example of Christian parents whose unmarried daughter became pregnant. It reflects pain, love, forgiveness and hope. I trust it will minister to you as it has to me.

Josh

Appendix

"Dad, I'm pregnant"

How Should a Father Respond?
(written by a distraught parent)

It seemed only yesterday that I was holding little Amy on my lap reading her bedtime stories. Now, with college classes and her extracurricular activities she had little time for old Dad. But this morning was different. She wanted to talk and I figured it must be about school, her job, or needing a loan.

She toyed with her food as my wife and I gave her time to gather her thoughts. Finally, she took a deep breath and said two words I thought I would never hear my unmarried teenage daughter say: "I'm pregnant."

It was as though an instant in time stood still. I was numb. Kay, my wife, picked up the conversation, "Are you sure?" Other such questions were asked, but I couldn't get my thoughts together to discuss it further. What was I to say? How should I respond and counsel my daughter?

Perhaps every parent struggles with the subconscious fear of their children engaging in premarital sex. Oh, there are those who court the idea that, "My kids are above average. I've taught them better and they're not really involved." They resist the thought that it may happen to them. But down deep

147

most parents are concerned that their children will become sexually active and, I believe, suffer with this same subconscious fear. It's tragic, but the fact is that your own son or daughter, your grandchild, your friend's child, or some of the kids at your church *are* sexually active on a consistent basis. And if one of them becomes pregnant, what will be your attitude? What will you say? What action will you take?

In this chapter, I would like to share the help I received from books, friends, and God's Word that guided my wife and me through this difficult period of our lives. My hope is that it can help youth directors, pastors, anyone with a friend in this situation and especially you parents who find yourselves struggling through the ordeal of an unmarried child's pregnancy.

The pregnancy of an unmarried girl is perhaps the most traumatic experience she will ever endure. She will probably feel she has lost everything she holds dear. She will be tempted to give in to such feelings as:

I've lost my past. "I have lost my morals and I am strapped with the social stigma of being an 'unmarried pregnant teenager.' I'll be looked upon by some as loose, immoral, and impure."

I've lost my freedom. "Now that I'm pregnant, there will be some things I won't be able to do physically. I may not feel comfortable going to work, church, and even shopping."

I've lost my future. "If I decide to keep the baby, the next 18 to 20 years of my life is planned. I will be making a commitment to my child, and my future will feel out of hand or pushed aside. As I feel less in control, I may feel pressured to marry."

I've lost my self-image. "As my body changes physically, it will be a constant reminder of what I've sacrificed. And I'll have a tendency to blame myself. I'll be tempted to take myself to task, think degrading things about myself, to punish myself emotionally for it."

I've lost my relationships. "How will family and friends feel about me? Boys may shy away from going out with me when they know I have a child. Family members and other adults who respected me before may not respect me now."

With these thoughts and emotions pouring down on her, it could cause some of these responses.

Grief. Experiencing these losses will undoubtedly bring pain and suffering and cause her to grieve over losing control of the life she had planned out.

Depression. If she doesn't obtain relief from her grief and suffering, she will go into depression and if depression is allowed to take over, she'll face despair and feel there is no hope—no light at the end of the tunnel.

Shame. Except for the grace of God, feelings of shame will affect her attitude toward herself, her friends, closest loved ones, and even toward the baby. Accepting feelings of shame is a devastating blow to her self-image and outlook on life. Shame can cloud every aspect of her life—work, school, caring for her child, working in the church, counseling and helping others.

If there is any time a girl needs the love, support, and wise counsel of her parents, it's during an unplanned pregnancy. But because parents equally experience a tremendous emotional turmoil, they risk the danger of negatively reacting rather than lovingly responding.

The next few days after learning of my daughter's pregnancy was one of the most emotional and confusing times of my life. Rarely do I shed tears, but that week I wept bitterly every day. I found myself negatively reacting to the entire situation. And if it hadn't been for dedicated counselors at the Crisis Pregnancy Center urging me to follow two very crucial principles, I would have probably driven my daughter to despair. These principles are what I'd like to share with you: 1) The power of forgiveness can untangle the emotions and clarify the thinking; and 2) Committing the future to God can provide a sense of direction.

My Need to Forgive

I sat in the counselor's office pouring out the hurt raging inside me. The counselor asked, "Why do you think you are hurting so?" "Well," I responded, "This whole ordeal is so painful. My little girl is hurting so much now and it's going to get a lot worse before it gets better. She'll suffer shame; may have to drop out of school; bear a child she can't provide for; and face other consequences I haven't even thought of." The counselor nodded slowly. I went on, "Amy has all these tough decisions to make. She'll have to decide whether to carry the baby to full term or abort the child (and thank God at this point Amy doesn't even consider abortion an appropriate option); decide about marrying Mark who fathered the child; decide whether to keep the baby or put the child up for adoption. And then there is her schooling. Should she go away to live with another family until the baby is born? There are so many variables within those questions that it boggles the mind, let alone the emotions. No matter what is done, everyone involved will feel the pain."

The wise counselor allowed me to wind down. After I finished, she leaned forward and said softly, "You say you have accepted Amy and aren't angry with her, but is the pain you feel all for your daughter?" I wasn't sure what she was driving at. "What do you mean?" I questioned. She continued. "I really encourage you to examine the reason for your personal hurt. Do you feel you have lost some of the things you wanted to share with your daughter?"

Yes, I had. Down deep *I too* suffered a loss. I wanted to give my lovely daughter as a virgin to a Christian young man. But I lost that. I wanted to experience the joy of my daughter's first child, but I couldn't have that either. I wanted to be a part of my first grandchild's life, but it appeared I had lost that opportunity too. My tears weren't just for Amy, they were for me too. I would also feel the shame and pain of her mistake.

I prayed for a spirit of forgiveness. Amy needed my support, love, and acceptance now more than ever. As I confessed my resentment and selfishness to God, He filled me with a supportive love for my daughter that I never thought possible. God's power of forgiveness took away the resentment. But there was more. My emotional confusion began to fade. The act of forgiving put the choices that would have to be made into perspective.

You see, the consequences of a few fleeting moments of uncontrolled passion seem endless. No matter which alternatives are considered, premature marriage, single parenting, or adoption—they are all painful and appear unacceptable. Confusion becomes the order of the day. Yet, when I found the power to forgive, I gained not only a supernatural supportive love for Amy, but a clarity of heart and mind to understand the alternatives. As my emotions untangled, I sat down and wrote her a long letter. Following are excerpts from that letter.

Dear Amy,

I know that during this past week you have suffered pain like never before, the burden that you bear is perhaps the heaviest you've ever carried. Yet through it all God assures us: "My grace is sufficient for you, for power is perfected in weakness" (2 Cor. 12:9).

And one thing I've come to realize is that God has not declared that life is over because of an unplanned pregnancy. God has great plans for your future. You have not been disqualified from the race. In fact, He plans to draw you closer to Him and teach you to know Him better than you have ever known Him before. Once we realize that our main purpose in life is to know God and glorify Him, life comes into proper perspective. And I believe, Amy, the more you and I know Him and see life from His perspective, the more life and all its struggles and problems begin to be resolved.

God has an answer for this situation. He has a solution. One without pain and suffering? Probably not. Yet, He has plenty of grace, that when appropriated to our lives, will be for our good and His glory. But, I've learned I can't appropriate His grace while responding to life in an unchristlike manner. So, I strive to " . . . stay always within the boundaries where God's love can reach and bless [me] you" (Jude 1:21 TLB). Once we begin to respond according to God's Word, we are then able to move on and *clearly understand the choices we have to make.*

I know you are struggling, even more than Mom and me, with a flood of emotions and it's difficult to think straight. I sense that this pregnancy represents the loss of everything you were holding dear. And while it may appear to be that way on the surface, you have not lost everything when you have God as your Savior and Friend. In fact, by properly responding to God and His Word, you will gain far more than you ever imagined.

Remember, Amy, you have sought God's forgiveness and that means your slate is clean—as far as God is concerned you've committed no sin, ever! Mom and I too have forgiven you. We can walk down the street with our daughter as proud as we've ever been. What makes us proud, and God too, is the fact that you've acknowledged your error, sought God's forgiveness, and committed your life to Him.

But what about the rest of your life? You have many difficult decisions to make. You have your life and the life of your baby to consider. There are no "perfect" answers. One of the things that makes this so difficult is that there are so many alternatives, and none of them are pleasant. But as you align your responses to the instructions of God's Word, the clouds will clear and He will make His will known.

I can't tell you what to do. You have engaged in an adult act and you have an adult decision to make. However, I want to point you to the context in which to make your decision. When you consider your options, do so with one central purpose in mind: "What will bring the most honor to God?"

Right choices will become clear as you (1) Maintain right attitudes (align yourself with God's Word during trying times, love those who mistreat·you, and accept your humbling position with grace); (2) Continue to consider only those options that would bring honor to God; and (3) Obtain wise counsel from mature Christians to confirm the leading you have.

If you decide to keep the baby, you can rest assured we will do all in our power to be the best grandparents possible. We will fill our responsibility in being a godly influence as best we can under God.

If you decide to relinquish the baby for adoption, you can

rest assured we will be there to support you, love you, weep with you, and heal together with you.

I love you dearly, Amy, more than you can know. You will always be my little girl. There are brighter and more beautiful days ahead for all of us. God will use this as a stepping stone in all our lives. We will learn much together. We can more effectively minister to others because of how we allow God to use this in our lives.

Through this we can all become even closer as a family than before. Mom and I really felt honored and want to thank you for sharing this with us on the very day you found out. We thank you for the opportunity to be a part of the decisions that affect the life of our first grandchild. No matter what, this will always be a special child to both of us and we have lots of love to share with you and your first child—in whatever way God chooses to let us be a part.

The road may seem dark and lonely at times, but remember we're always here and want to help. And more importantly, Christ is with you always, your dearest Friend, your closest companion, the One who knows you most and loves you best. Mom and I pray for you daily. I love you, I love you, I love you.

Your Dad

My Need to Commit the Future to God

Amy had more than seven months to make the biggest decision of her life. She was confident that marrying Mark would further complicate matters. We agreed. But was she to rear her child as a single parent? Or, were we to assume the responsibility of rearing our first grandchild? Or, did God have a Christian couple prepared to rear our daughter's baby? Weeks turned into months and still no clear direction. We prayed daily that God would provide clear direction to Amy.

One afternoon while discussing the options with her, she became frustrated. "Dad," she said in tears, "I've got to know what's right to do. Why won't you tell me what I should do?"

My eyes blurred as I tried to explain, "Amy, you know that I love you. And I want what is best for you and the baby." My voice choked with emotion. "I *could* tell you what was right if I could only see some twenty years into the future, but I can't. Honey, I don't know exactly what to do either, but I do know how you can find out." She sobbed quietly as I went on. "Commit your future into God's hands who does know the future—give *Him* your baby, relinquish that life within you into His care. Once so committed, ask *Him* what *He* wants to do with *His* little unborn child. Tell God you are gladly willing to rear your baby if He so desires, and you are equally willing for Him to hand your child to another to rear."

As weeks went by, God gave Amy the ability to relinquish her child and her own future into His hands. Slowly pieces of the puzzle came together. One confirmation after another made it clear to her, and eventually to all of us, what she was to do. I hesitate to share her decision simply because I would not want it to be considered a determining factor for anyone else. Each family situation is unique and must be considered separately before God. However, I believe the principle is applicable to all: Commit your future and the life of the baby to God and He will direct you.

With caution I share that God did direct Amy to a couple, we believe to be of God's choosing, to rear our first granddaughter. Watching my daughter place my first grandchild in the arms of a friend to later present to the new adoptive parents was the most bittersweet moment of my life. I could have never withstood the pain of it all, if I too had not first turned my granddaughter over to God.

As I look back over the year, I see that actually I offered very little advice to my daughter, but did give lots of love and support. And it was that love and support from both Kay and me that allowed what little counsel we did offer to be of such help.

If you find yourself in a similar situation, I urge you to seek God's grace early and the support of wise biblical counselors. Transparently confess the pain and hurt you feel. Allow

God to fill you with the power of His forgiveness and then commit the future of your daughter and her baby into His hands. I'm confident that God makes His will known to those who honestly and unselfishly seek his leadership.

The bitter consequences of an unplanned pregnancy in the life of an unmarried girl and her family is beyond my ability to describe here. God certainly knew what was best when He commanded against premarital sex. Our entire ordeal causes us to praise God for His specific moral commands of love. They are commands designed for the protection and provision of young people. But perhaps even more than that, we praise God for being the gracious Forgiver and loving Friend who lifts the fallen and restores a broken life. He was there through every moment of every day drawing my daughter to His soothing breast. In the lonely night hours of pain and regret, He was there; during the times of indecision and confusion, He was there; and in the final moments of seeing our only granddaughter taken away, oh, He was there. You see, He too knows the pain of giving up a child. "For God so loved . . . that He gave His only Son." And He was there to carry us through. He'll be there for you, too, if you ever find yourself in a similar situation. To God be the glory!

JOSH McDOWELL is one of the most articulate and popular youth speakers today, having spoken to more than seven million young people in seventy-four countries. A graduate of Wheaton College and a magna cum laude graduate of Talbot Theological Seminary, he is the author of twenty-eight books, and has been featured in twenty-one films and two television specials. Among his most popular books are *Evidence That Demands a Verdict, The Resurrection Factor, More Than a Carpenter,* and *Evidence for Joy.* His film series, *Evidence for Faith,* is a classic in the field of popular apologetics. Josh has been a traveling representative for Campus Crusade for Christ for twenty-five years, heads the Josh McDowell Ministries international organization, and is resident instructor at the Julian Center, a campus in the mountains near San Diego, offering a unique three-month discipleship experience. Josh and his wife, Dottie, live in Julian, California, with their four children.

Strommen, Merton P. *Five Cries of Youth*. New York: Harper & Row, 1974.

Strommen, Merton P. and Strommen, Irene. *Five Cries of Parents*. New York: Harper & Row, 1985.

Swindoll, Charles. *You and Your Child*. Hodder & Stoughton, 1984.

Ziglar, Zig. *Raising Positive Kids in a Negative World*. Kingsway, 1986.